D0095971

Basic Catechism

"With the publication of the eighth revised edition of the *Basic Catechism*, Pauline Books & Media has once again provided us with a doctrinally-sound and reader-friendly basic resource for anyone seeking to learn (more) about the Catholic faith. This is a great tool, especially for use by parents and catechists."

— ✠ Richard J. Malone, Th.D., S.T.L., Bishop of Buffalo

"The Catholic faith is big, beautiful, and mysterious. We can often feel like travelers in a strange land as we explore it. Sr. Mary Lea Hill, FSP, provides a wonderful service for both converts and cradle Catholics alike in this accessible guidebook for the wonderers and adventurers who seek to answer the call of Jesus from the heart of the Church."

— Mark P. Shea, author of *Salt and Light: The Commandments, the Beatitudes, and a Joyful Life*

"Anyone looking for information on the Catholic faith needs a copy of *Basic Catechism*. This handy, easy-to-read book covers the Creed, Sacraments, morality, and prayer. Complete with Scripture citations, cross-references to the *Catechism of the Catholic Church*, and an index, this popular handbook will provide you with whatever you need to know about the Catholic Church."

— Sr. Lorraine Trouvé, FSP, writer for the "Ask a Catholic Nun" Facebook page and editor of *Basic Catechism*

"Do we need another basic catechism? This one we do. Sister Mary Lea Hill, FSP, and Sister Helen Wallace, FSP, give us a comprehensive explanation of the Catholic faith and a guide to living a faith-filled Catholic life. As expected, answers are annotated to the appropriate *Catechism of the Catholic Church* paragraphs as well as Scripture references. Sections on Sacraments and Commandments stand out with a richness that will benefit the scholar, the seeker, and all in between. The detailed but easy-to-read description of the Mass, and the vestments and vessels at Mass, make this an ideal reference for RCIA groups, but it belongs on the shelf of any serious Catholic."

— Susan Abbott, Director, Office of Religious Education,
Archdiocese of Boston

Basic Catechism

FAQs About the Catholic Faith

Eighth Revised Edition

In accordance with the
Catechism of the Catholic Church

Mary Lea Hill, FSP
and Susan Helen Wallace, FSP

auline
BOOKS & MEDIA

Nihil Obstat: Reverend Thomas W. Buckley, S.T.D., S.S.L.

Imprimatur: ✠ Seán Cardinal O'Malley, O.F.M. Cap.
Archbishop of Boston
October 26, 2012

Library of Congress Cataloging-in-Publication Data

Hill, Mary Lea.
  Basic catechism : FAQS about the Catholic faith / Mary Lea Hill, FSP, and Susan Helen Wallace, FSP. -- Eighth revised edition in accordance with the Catechism of the Catholic Church.
    pages cm
  Rev. ed. of: Basic catechism / Daughters of St. Paul. 7th rev. ed. c1999.
  Includes index.
  ISBN-13: 978-0-8198-1205-6
  ISBN-10: 0-8198-1205-6
  1. Catholic Church--Catechisms--English. 2. Catholic Church--Catechisms. I. Title.
  BX1961.B29 2013
  238'.2--dc23

2012048228

Published by Pauline Books & Media, 50 Saint Pauls Avenue, Boston, MA 02130-3491

Printed in the U.S.A.

www.pauline.org

Pauline Books & Media is the publishing house of the Daughters of St. Paul, an international congregation of women religious serving the Church with the communications media.

1 2 3 4 5 6 7 8 9   17 16 15 14 13

Contents

INTRODUCTORY NOTE .... *xi*

THE PROFESSION OF FAITH *1*

How We Know About God *3*

What Is God Like? *12*

God Our Creator *16*

Why Are We on This Earth? *25*

God Sends His Son *28*

Belief in the Holy Spirit *45*

Belief in the Holy Catholic Church *48*

The Mystery of the Church *48*

Christ's Faithful: Hierarchy, Laity, Consecrated Life *52*

Life Everlasting *65*

THE CELEBRATION OF THE CHRISTIAN MYSTERY *73*

The Liturgy *75*

The Sacraments: Actions of Jesus *79*

Sacraments of Christian Initiation *83*

Baptism *83*

Confirmation *92*

Eucharist *96*

Sacraments of Healing 117

    Penance and Reconciliation 117

    Indulgences 127

    Anointing of the Sick 130

Sacraments at the Service of Communion 134

    Holy Orders 134

    Matrimony 139

Sacramentals 150

LIFE IN CHRIST 155

The Dignity of the Human Person 157

Conscience 163

Virtue 167

Personal Sin 175

The Ten Commandments 181

    First Commandment 183

    Second Commandment 190

    Third Commandment 194

    Fourth Commandment 197

    Fifth Commandment 201

    Sixth Commandment 211

    Seventh Commandment 218

    Eighth Commandment 225

    Ninth Commandment 231

    Tenth Commandment 234

    Some Special Duties of Catholic Christians 235

CHRISTIAN PRAYER 241

    Prayer: Communication with God 243

    The Lord's Prayer 249

    The Hail Mary and the Rosary 253

APPENDICES 255

    1. Prayers 257

    2. Guidelines for Christian Living 264

    3. The Books of the Bible 268

INDEX 271

Introductory Note

This eighth edition of the *Basic Catechism* has been expanded and revised to more closely reflect the Church's teaching on the challenges facing the faithful Christian in today's society. It also reflects changes in the liturgy due to the new translation of the Mass texts that took effect in Advent 2011. The material is divided according to the four sections of the *Catechism of the Catholic Church*: the profession of faith, the celebration of the Christian mystery, life in Christ, and Christian prayer.

The numbers in parentheses that follow the questions refer to related paragraphs in the *Catechism of the Catholic Church*. Together with the index, these cross-references will direct the reader to further information on particular topics. A section of basic prayers and guidelines for Christian living serves as a convenient reference.

THE PROFESSION OF FAITH

How We Know About God

Does God exist?

Yes, God exists.

One God and Father of us all, who is above all, through all, and in all. (Eph 4:6)

Who is God?

God is the all-powerful Spirit who created everything that exists. He is our Father who is with us always and awaits us in heaven to share his everlasting joys with us. (205–221)

For God who made the world and everything in it—the Lord of the heavens and the earth—does not dwell in sanctuaries made by human hands, nor does he need anything we can do for him since he gives everyone life and breath and everything. (Acts 17:24)

How can we know that God exists?

Through reason and revelation we can know that God exists. (35)

What is reason?

Reason is our power to think. (33)

What are some of the ways God's existence can be known by our power to think and reason?

We can know about God's existence from nature's laws and purposes, the degrees of perfection in the universe, motion,

causes and effects, and the order and design of the universe.
The longings of the human heart, conscience, and freedom
point to God as the ultimate source of our happiness. (31–35)

The Bible puts this question to us:

> *For if they had the power to know so much that they could investigate the world, how did they fail to find sooner the* Lord *of these things?* (Wis 13:9)

What arguments do the "new" atheists offer against belief in God?

They offer arguments such as these to disprove God's existence: Religion opposes progress and freedom by encouraging
a demeaning acceptance of suffering and suppression; religion
promotes dissension and thus evil, violence, and abuse; religion
negates personal maturity with a primitive, superstitious delusion; and religion pits irrational speculation against scientific
evidence.

Does the universe itself point to a Creator?

Yes, in its magnificence and order the universe points to a
Creator. St. Paul says:

> *From the creation of the world God's invisible attributes—his eternal power and divine nature—have been accessible to human knowledge through what can be perceived, and so they have no excuse.* (Rom 1:20. See also Rom 11:36.) (32, 36)

What other religious facts can we know by our reason?

Some religious facts we can know by our reason are:
- ❖ the human soul will never die (366);
- ❖ everyone has a duty to worship God, who created us (2096, 2135);
- ❖ the historical character of the Gospels makes them worthy of being believed (514–515).

What is God's revelation?

God's revelation is what he has told us about himself, ourselves, and his plan of love for us. Revelation is God's self-communication to us, which he has made known to us through Scripture and Tradition, as taught by the teaching authority of the Church. (50–51, 80)

> *Of old God spoke to our fathers through the prophets many times and in various ways, but in these last days he has spoken to us through a Son. . . .* (Heb 1:1–2)

Why do we need God's revelation?

We need God's revelation because without his help our reason could not discover everything that God wants us to know about himself, ourselves, and his plan of love for us now and in the life to come. (37–38, 52)

How has God given us his revelation?

God has made himself known to us through his deeds and words in salvation history. He gave us the fullness of revelation in his Son, Jesus Christ, who is God-made-man. This revelation comes to us through Scripture and Tradition, as interpreted by the Church. (74–87, 95)

What is Sacred Tradition?

Sacred Tradition is the process by which the Church, through the assistance of the Holy Spirit, preserves and hands on to all generations, in its teaching, life, and worship, all that it is and all that it believes. (78)

> *But there are also many other things that Jesus did; if every one of them were written down, I suppose the world itself could not contain the books that would be written.* (Jn 21:25)

How important is Sacred Tradition?

Sacred Tradition is of prime importance because in it we have certainty about the things we must believe and do. (80–81)

> *Stand firm and hold fast to the tradition we taught you, whether by word of mouth or by a letter of ours.* (2 Thes 2:15)

What is meant by the "heritage of faith"?

The "heritage of faith" (sometimes called the "deposit of faith") means the truths which God has revealed and has given to the Church to keep and to teach. This should not be thought of in a static sense, since the Church grows in understanding this heritage of faith. (84–95, 175)

What is the Bible?

The Bible is the book which contains the inspired word of God. In it God speaks to us through the writings of human authors whom he chose and whom the Holy Spirit guided. (81)

> *Thus says the LORD, the God of Israel: Write in a book all the words that I have spoken to you.* (Jer 30:2)

What are other names for the Bible?

The Bible is also called "Sacred Scripture," which means "holy writings," or just "Scriptures," or "the word of God," since it is God's revelation to us.

What are the main parts of the Bible?

The main parts of the Bible are the Old Testament, the forty-six books written before the birth of Jesus, and the New Testament, the twenty-seven books written after Jesus' resurrection. (120) These books are listed in the *Guidelines for Christian Living* (see p. 268).

What is the Bible's main theme?

The Bible's main theme is God's saving love for us human beings, even though we are sinful.

What is divine inspiration?

Divine inspiration is the special guidance the Holy Spirit gave to the Bible's human authors, so that they wrote everything God wanted and only that, without error. (105–106)

> *All Scripture is inspired by God and is useful for teaching, reproving, correcting, and training in righteousness, so that the man of God may be fully capable of carrying out every good work.* (2 Tm 3:16–17)

What is the Old Testament about?

The Old Testament tells the history of God's saving actions in the lives of the chosen people, the Israelites, through whom God brought about his plan of salvation. (122)

> *Salvation is from the Jews.* (Jn 4:22)

Briefly, what is the history of the Chosen People?

Their history began with Abraham, whom God called to be father and leader of the Chosen People. Later Moses was sent to free the people from slavery in Egypt and to give them the Ten Commandments, which God had revealed to him. God chose Joshua to lead the people into Canaan, the "Promised Land." Later David became a great king of Israel and an ancestor of Christ. God sent prophets such as Isaiah and Jeremiah to speak his words to the people and encourage them to grow in fidelity to the covenant. At one point, God permitted the destruction of the center of worship, Jerusalem, and the exile of its people into Babylon. The exiles who later returned to Jerusalem rebuilt the temple and renewed the covenant. (59–64)

What is the New Testament about?

The New Testament is about the birth, life, teachings, death, and resurrection of Jesus Christ, the Son of God, as well as the life and growth of the early Church which he founded. (124)

> *The appointed time has come and the kingdom of God is at hand; repent and believe in the Good News!* (Mk 1:15)

What is the Gospel?

The Gospel or "Good News" consists of the first four books of the New Testament and gives us a detailed description of the life and teachings of Jesus. For Christians, these four books are the most important books of the Bible. (125)

What do we learn from the Gospels?

From the Gospels we learn what Jesus asks us to believe and do in order to be saved and reach heaven. We learn about the great love Jesus and his Father have for us. Because of this love Jesus died for us, to redeem us from our sins. (125)

> *What we have seen and heard we also proclaim to you so you too may be in fellowship with us. Our fellowship is with the Father and with his Son, Jesus Christ, and we are writing these things so that our joy may be complete.* (1 Jn 1:3–4)

How did the four Gospels come to be written?

The Gospels were formed through a three-stage process: (a) the life and ministry of Jesus; (b) the oral preaching of the apostles, who proclaimed what Jesus had done and taught; (c) the writing of the Gospels. The evangelists drew on the oral tradition to give their specific audiences an account of Jesus' saving deeds. (126)

Can people make mistakes when they try to understand the Bible?

Difficulties in translating and interpreting the language, customs, and history of the times can lead to misunderstanding biblical texts. One of the reasons Jesus gave us the Church is to guide us in reading the Bible. (109–119)

Jesus said to them, "Is this not the reason you go astray, that you understand neither the Scriptures nor the power of God?" (Mk 12:24)

There are some things in his [St. Paul's] letters which are difficult to understand—ignorant and unstable people distort them, just as they distort the other scriptures, to their own destruction! (2 Pt 3:16)

Can the Church make a mistake in interpreting the Bible?

The Church can never make a mistake in authentically interpreting the Bible because the Holy Spirit preserves the Church from error. (85–87)

What does the Church consider in interpreting the Bible?

The Church considers the tradition of the Church Fathers and Doctors, the original languages, literary forms, the actual text, and historical findings. This helps to reach the true meaning which the sacred author, under divine inspiration, had in writing and to avoid a purely fundamentalist view which can be a false interpretation. (111–114)

What is the difference between the Catholic Bible and those of other Christian denominations?

There are two main differences: first, the number of books of the Bible accepted as inspired by God is different, and second, the interpretation of certain teachings in the Bible differ, as found in study notes.

What is the reason for these differences?

These differences resulted from biblical scholarship and theology within Catholic and Protestant tradition. While we respect the beliefs of the different churches and show reverence for the Bible in every form, as Catholics we trust in the Catholic biblical teaching because of our belief in the Holy Spirit's guidance.

How is the Bible to be read?

The Bible is to be read humbly and prayerfully, with a readiness to put God's word into practice. (131–133)

What is faith?

Faith is a gift from God by which we believe what he has revealed. By faith the whole person adheres to God in a free response of loving trust. (91, 153–155, 176–184)

Now it is impossible to please God without faith, because to even approach God you have to believe that God exists and that he rewards those who seek him. (Heb 11:6)

What is the Profession of Faith we recite at Mass?

The Profession of Faith we recite at Mass is either the Nicene Creed, an ancient declaration of belief in the principal truths of faith, or the Apostles' Creed, which is especially used during Lent and Easter. (195)

Who are the faithful?

The faithful are loyal followers of the Lord Jesus. They share in his priestly, prophetic, and royal office through their Baptism. (871–873)

Symeon Peter, a servant and apostle of Jesus Christ, to those who have received a faith of equal worth with ours through the saving will of our God and the Savior Jesus Christ: may grace and peace abound to you through knowledge of God and Jesus our Lord. (2 Pt 1:1–2)

What Is God Like?

Is God perfect?

Yes, God is perfect. He is almighty, eternal, all-present, all-good, all-knowing, all-merciful, and all-just. (213)

Nor does he need anything we can do for him since he gives everyone life and breath and everything. (Acts 17:25)

What do we mean when we say that God is almighty, eternal, merciful, and just?

Almighty means all-powerful.

And you rule over all. In your hand are power and might; and it is in your hand to make great and to give strength to all. (1 Chr 29:12)

Eternal means "outside of time"—without beginning or end—and unchanging. (220)

For a thousand years in your sight are like yesterday when it is past, or like a watch in the night. (Ps 90:4)

Merciful means loving and forgiving.

Be merciful, as your Father is merciful. (Lk 6:36)

Just means fair.

Just and true are your ways, King of nations! (Rev 15:3)

What word describes God's unlimited perfection?

God's unlimited perfection is *infinite*.

But for God all things are possible. (Mt 19:26)

Does God change?

No, God does not change. (212, 227)

. . . in whom there is no variation or darkness due to change. (Jas 1:17)

What does the name YHWH tell us about God?

The Hebrew name YHWH, meaning "I AM WHO AM," tells us that God is life itself. (206, 213)

God said to Moses, "I AM WHO I AM." And he said, "Say this to the people of Israel, 'I AM has sent me to you'. . . this is my name for ever. . . ." (Ex 3:14–15)

Does God care about us?

Yes, God cares about us. His loving action in our lives is called Divine Providence. (302–314)

If I take the wings of the morning and settle at the farthest limits of the sea, even there your hand shall lead me, and your right hand shall hold me fast. (Ps 139:9–10)

What is a mystery?

In religion a mystery is a great truth revealed by God which our limited intelligence will never be able to wholly understand. (42–43, 48)

What special mystery has God told us about himself?

God has told us about the mystery of the Blessed Trinity. He has revealed himself to be three Persons in one God—our *Triune God.* (234, 237)

Go, therefore, and make disciples of all nations, baptizing them in the name of the Father and of the Son and of the Holy Spirit. . . . (Mt 28:19)

Chosen according to the foreknowledge of God the Father through sanctification by the Spirit for obedience to Jesus Christ. . . . (1 Pt 1:2)

What is the mystery of the Blessed Trinity?

The mystery of the Blessed Trinity is that there are three divine Persons—Father, Son, and Holy Spirit—in the one, true God. (233, 253–255)

> *The grace of the Lord Jesus Christ, the love of God, and the fellowship of the Holy Spirit be with you all.* (2 Cor 13:13)

Is the Father God?

The Father is God and the First Person of the Blessed Trinity. (240, 262)

Is the Son God?

The Son is God and the Second Person of the Blessed Trinity. (240–242)

Is the Holy Spirit God?

The Holy Spirit is God and the Third Person of the Blessed Trinity. (243)

Can we understand anything about the mystery of the Blessed Trinity?

We can understand that by "one God" we mean the one divine nature, while by "three Persons" we mean the Father, Son, and Holy Spirit, who each totally possess the divine nature. (253–256)

> *One Lord, one faith, one baptism, one God and Father of us all, who is above all, through all, and in all.* (Eph 4:4–6)

What is the importance of the mystery of the Blessed Trinity for our own lives?

The three Persons of the Trinity call us to everlasting happiness with them. At Baptism they came to live within us. If we grow in grace through the sacraments and virtuous living, we will draw closer to our Triune God throughout life and will share eternal union with the Trinity in heaven. (257–260)

> *I bend my knees to the Father. From him every family in the heavens and on earth is named, so that from the riches of his glory he may grant you inner strength and power through his Spirit. May Christ dwell in your hearts through faith, firmly rooted and established in love, so that with all the saints you may be able to understand the breadth, the length, the height, and depth, and know Christ's love which surpasses all knowledge so that you may be filled with all God's fullness.* (Eph 3:14–19)

God Our Creator

Who is the Father?

The Father is the First Person of the Blessed Trinity, who is also called the Creator. (238, 239, 279)

In the beginning God created the heavens and the earth. (Gen 1:1)

Why is God called "Father"?

We call God "Father" because he is the Creator of all, above all, and yet concerned about all that he has made. We know God as "Father" because that is how he revealed himself and Jesus referred to God as his "Father." (238, 240)

All things have been given to me by my Father. . . . (Mt 11:27)

Is God also "Mother"?

God is a being far superior to our understanding. Unlike creatures God is neither male nor female; God is God. However, since all fatherhood and motherhood has its source in God, we can say that God possesses all the qualities of both father and mother. (239)

As one whom his mother comforts, so I will comfort you. (Is 66:13)

What does "create" mean?

To create means to bring something out of nothing. (286, 296–298, 327)

Through faith we understand that the world was created by the word of God, so that what is seen came to be from what cannot be seen. (Heb 11:3)

What did God create?

God created all the matter and energy in the universe, as well as the pure spirits called angels and the soul of each one of us. (290, 299)

All things came to be through him, and without him nothing came to be. (Jn 1:3)

Why did God create the world?

God created the world out of goodness, to show us his perfections and to share them with us. (288, 293–295)

What came to be through him was life, and the life was the light of men. (Jn 1:3–4)

What are angels?

Angels are spirits, that is, real spiritual beings without bodies, possessing understanding and free will. (328–330)

Bless the LORD, O you his angels, you mighty ones who do his word, hearkening to the voice of his word! (Ps 103:20)

Can we prove from reason alone that angels exist?

We cannot prove from reason alone that angels exist, yet their existence is not contrary to reason. It is very "reasonable" to suggest that just as there are creatures composed totally of matter, and creatures made up of matter and spirit, so there are purely spiritual creatures. For this belief we rely on the testimony of Scripture and the Fathers of the Church. (328)

Praise him, all his angels, praise him, all his host! (Ps 148:2)

How many angels are there?

The exact number of angels is unknown, but the Bible tells us that many exist. In the garden of Gethsemane, Jesus said:

Or do you think that I could not call on my Father and have him at once send me more than twelve legions of angels? (Mt 26:53) (See also Dn 7:10.)

Did God bestow certain gifts on the angels in creating them?

God gave special gifts of grace, wisdom, power, and holiness to the angels. They were also given the opportunity to merit the direct vision of God by remaining faithful to him.

They are not afraid to blaspheme heavenly beings, whereas angels who are much greater in power and might do not denounce them in such insulting terms before the Lord. (2 Pt 2:11)

Did every angel remain faithful to God?

Not all of the angels remained faithful to God; some "radically and irrevocably *rejected* God and his reign." (392)

For if God did not spare the angels when they sinned . . . then the Lord is able to . . . keep the wicked under punishment for the day of judgment. (2 Pt 2:4, 9) (See also Jude 6.)

What reward was granted to the faithful angels?

The faithful angels were admitted to God's presence where they see him face to face. These good angels see, love, and adore God, and live with him eternally. (329)

Their angels in heaven continually look upon the face of my Father in heaven. (Mt 18:10)

Do the good angels help us?

The good angels help us especially by praying for us and by being our guardian angels. (334–335)

For a good angel will go with him. (Tob 5:21) (See also Heb 1:14.)

Who are the guardian angels?

The guardian angels are pure spirits who watch over us and encourage us to lead good Christian lives. (336)

The angel of the LORD encamps around those who fear him, and delivers them. (Ps 34:7)

Who are archangels?

Archangels are members of a very powerful group of angels. From the Bible we know the names of three: Michael, Raphael, and Gabriel. (335)

The Lord himself will come down from heaven and issue a command, with an archangel's voice and a blast from God's trumpet. (1 Thes 4:16)

What happened to the unfaithful angels?

The unfaithful angels who rebelled against God were banished from his presence to the eternal punishment known as hell. They are called devils or evil spirits. (391)

Get away from me, you cursed, into the eternal fire prepared for the Devil and his angels. . . . (Mt 25:41)

Do the unfaithful angels try to harm us?

The unfaithful angels try to harm us chiefly by tempting us to sin. (395, 407–409)

Your adversary the Devil goes about like a roaring lion seeking someone to devour. (1 Pt 5:8) (See also Mt 10:1; Eph 6:11.)

Do all of our temptations to sin come from the unfaithful angels?

Only some of our temptations to sin come from the unfaithful angels. Other temptations come from ourselves, our wounded nature, or from other persons and things about us. (1264)

> *When I want to do what is right, evil awaits me, for although I agree with God's law in my inmost self I can see that there is another law in my bodily members which wars against the law of my reason and holds me captive to the law of sin in my bodily members.* (Rom 7:21–23. See also Jas 1:13–14; 1 Jn 2:15.)

Are we always able to resist all temptations?

Yes, because no matter how powerful temptations may be, they are not sins in themselves. God will always give us grace and strength if we ask him.

> *So anyone who thinks they are standing should he careful not to fall. The only temptations you have received are normal human ones. God is trustworthy and does not test us beyond our strength— along with the temptation he will also provide a way out, so you will be able to endure it.* (1 Cor 10:12–13)

What is a human person?

Created in the image and likeness of God, the human person is a union of body and soul, endowed with intelligence and freedom, who will live forever. (355–358, 362–368)

> *It was he who created man in the beginning, and he left him in the power of his own inclination.* (Sir 15:14)

After creating us, does God leave us on our own?

God continues to love and care for us. Without his activity in our lives we could not think, decide, or act. By his power God keeps the whole universe from returning to nothingness (see 2 Mc 7:28). We call God's action his divine Providence. Creation is just the beginning of God's saving actions in the world and in our own lives. (300, 304)

> *Many are the plans in the mind of a man, but it is the purpose of the LORD that will be established.* (Prov 19:21)

What is the significance of the Sabbath in the work of creation?

God worked at creation for six "days." He blessed the seventh "day" as a day of rest, a day for praise and worship. By giving us this day of rest, God teaches us to reflect on the beauty of all creation, to respect his plan of creation by faithfully observing the laws he has established, and to worship and adore his goodness. (345–347)

So God blessed the seventh day and hallowed it, because on it God rested from all his work which he had done in creation. (Gen 2:3)

What are the main facts to know about creation?

God created all matter and energy in the universe; if there was evolution, God planned and guided it; and every human soul is created directly by God at the moment of the conception of the body.

And the dust returns to the earth as it was, and the spirit returns to God who gave it. (Eccl 12:7)

What is the theory of evolution?

The theory of evolution proposes that the universe, as we know it today, is the product of a chain of development. The Church neither subscribes to this theory nor condemns it. The Catholic belief, however, is that even if the human body was formed through an evolving process, each human soul is created directly by God.

What is the greatest glory God receives in the visible universe?

Although the whole universe reflects the infinite wisdom, beauty, and goodness of the Creator, the greatest glory God receives in the visible universe comes from human persons.

Only human persons have the freedom to choose to love, adore, and serve the Creator. (342–343, 356)

> *Are not five sparrows sold for a few cents? Yet not one of these is overlooked in the presence of God! On the contrary, even the hairs of your head are all numbered. Fear not! You are worth far more than sparrows.* (Lk 12:6–7)

Who were the first man and woman?

The first man and woman, the first parents of the entire human race, are known as Adam and Eve. (375) (See Gen 1–4.)

Must we believe in the existence of Adam and Eve?

While belief in a single set of original parents may be difficult in view of scientific theories of the beginning of our species, we must hold to the belief that God directly willed and created the first humans. The Genesis story of creation must be respected as the interpretation chosen by God.

What was the mastery or "dominion" that our first parents exercised over creation?

Because God created Adam and Eve in the divine image and likeness, he placed them in charge of the rest of creation to care for it. (307, 373, 377–378)

> *And God blessed them, and God said to them, "Be fruitful and multiply, and fill the earth and subdue it; and have dominion."* (Gen 1:28)

What other gifts did our first parents receive from God?

God gave them natural goodness and happiness, God's friendship or grace, inner harmony, as well as harmony with nature, knowledge, self-control, and freedom from suffering and death. This harmonious and blessed existence is known as the state of "original justice." (374–376)

Were Adam and Eve capable of sinning?

Adam and Eve were capable of sinning because God gave them free will. (387)

And if you are unwilling to serve the LORD, choose this day whom you will serve. . . . (Josh 24:15)

What does it mean to sin?

To sin means to reject or oppose God or his law knowingly and willfully. (386–387)

For whoever knows what he should do and does not do it is committing a sin. (Jas 4:17)

Did Adam and Eve sin?

They sinned when they freely disobeyed a direct command of God. (379, 397)

God said, "You shall not eat of the fruit of the tree which is in the midst of the garden. . . ." When the woman saw that the tree was good for food, and that is was a delight to the eyes, and that the tree was to be desired to make one wise, she took of its fruit and ate; and she also gave some to her husband, and he ate. (Gen 3:3, 6)

What happened to our first parents because of their sin?

They lost the grace of holiness, their friendship with God, their inner harmony, the right to heaven, and the other gifts they had received. They became subject to suffering and death, felt strong inclinations to evil, and were forced out of the garden of paradise. (399–401)

Therefore the Lord GOD sent him forth from the garden of Eden. . . . (Gen 3:23)

Does the sin of our first parents have any effect on us, their descendants?

Because of their sin, we are born without sanctifying grace and inherit Adam's punishment, as we would have inherited his gifts had he been faithful to God. (390, 402)

> *Therefore, just as through one man sin entered the world, and through sin, death, and in this way death spread to all men. . . .* (Rom 5:12)

What is this sin in us called?

This sin in us is called original sin.

How did the sin of Adam and Eve become our sin?

The transmission of original sin is a mystery. It is not a personal sin on our part; however, we inherit their weakened and sinful human nature. "Original sin is called 'sin' only in an analogical sense: it is a sin 'contracted' and not 'committed'—a state and not an act," says the *Catechism of the Catholic Church*. (404)

Do we have to believe in original sin?

Belief in the reality of original sin is essential to our understanding and appreciation of our redemption by Christ. Having sinned in Adam, we need redemption in Christ. (388–389)

> *So then, just as one man's offense resulted in condemnation for all, so too one man's obedience resulted in pardon and life for all.* (Rom 5:19)

Was anyone ever free from original sin?

Jesus' Mother Mary, in view of the merits of her divine Son, was preserved from original sin from the moment of her conception in her mother's womb. This great privilege is called the Immaculate Conception. (491)

> *Hail, full of grace, the Lord is with you!* (Lk 1:28)

Why Are We on This Earth?

What is the purpose of our life on earth?

The purpose of our life on earth is to attain the everlasting happiness found only in God. (356–358)

God gave us eternal life, and this life is in his Son. (1 Jn 5:11)

Why can only God make us happy?

God gave us such a great desire for happiness that nothing less than union with him can satisfy us.

Blessed is every one who fears the LORD, who walks in his ways! . . . You shall be happy, and it shall be well with you. (Ps 128:1–2)

Will this happiness come to us automatically?

No, because we possess intelligence and free will, God asks us to cooperate with him by knowing, loving, and serving him. (27)

Set about accomplishing your salvation with fear and trembling. (Phil 2:12)

How can we know God?

With our reason, we can come to know something about God through the created world. But this knowledge can be hard to attain, so God has revealed himself to us. He did this through his saving deeds and words in the history of Israel, and then by sending his Son, Jesus Christ, who is the fullness of revelation. Jesus's teaching comes to us through Scripture and Sacred Tradition, as taught and interpreted by the Church. In Baptism we receive the gift of the Holy Spirit who enables us to believe through faith. (31–38, 50–67)

> *His invisible attributes of eternal power and divinity have been able to be understood and perceived in what he has made.* (Rom 1:20)

How can we love and serve God?

We can love and serve God mainly by wanting to love and serve him, avoiding sin, sharing in the sacraments, especially Penance and Eucharist, remaining loyal to the teachings and laws of Christ's Church, drawing others to God by living a Christ-like life, and frequent prayer.

When can we share in God's happiness?

We can begin to share in God's happiness now by living good lives, which bring peace of heart. But by far the greatest happiness will be enjoyed after death. Then the faithful person will hear:

> *Well done, good and faithful servant! You were faithful over a few things, so now I will set you over many. Come into your master's joy!* (Mt 25:23)

Does every human being live on after death?

The human soul is immortal. At the resurrection from the dead at the end of the world, body and soul will be reunited to live forever. (997–998, 1022)

> *. . . those who did good deeds to the resurrection of life, but those who wrought evil to the resurrection of judgment.* (Jn 5:29)

Do we have a name for this everlasting happiness with God?

"Heaven is the ultimate end and fulfillment of the deepest human longings, the state of supreme, definitive happiness," states the *Catechism of the Catholic Church*. (1024)

Right now we see indistinctly, as in a mirror, but then we will see face to face. (1 Cor 13:12)

How do we know that heaven exists?

God has told us that heaven exists; Jesus spoke many times of the eternal reward that awaits the just. (1027)

Then the righteous will shine like the sun in the kingdom of their Father. (Mt 13:43)

Is it important to keep heaven in mind?

The thought of heaven gives us hope; it helps us to be happier, to lead better lives, and to do more good.

Whoever sows bountifully will also reap bountifully. . . . God loves a cheerful giver . . . and is able to provide you with every gift so that you will always have enough of everything and will have more than enough for every good work. (2 Cor 9:6–8)

God Sends His Son

What is salvation history?

Salvation history is the story of God's loving action in the lives of human beings to free them from sin and to bring them to himself.

Do we have a part in salvation history?

We can cooperate with God's loving plan by sharing in the life of grace which he makes available to us through the Church.

What are the greatest of God's saving actions?

The Incarnation, death, and resurrection of Jesus, God's only-begotten Son, are his greatest saving actions, through which our redemption was accomplished.

When did salvation history start?

Salvation history started at the time of our first parents, who sinned seriously and lost God's grace for themselves and their descendants. Sin began to spread in the world, but God did not abandon the human race. He continually offered a covenant to us and through the prophets taught us about his great love for us. When the right time came, God sent his Son to die for our sins and lead us to eternal life.

Now, by the working of the Holy Spirit, God continues to bring to all people the salvation that Jesus won for us on Calvary's cross. (54ff.)

With every manner of wisdom and understanding he made known to us the mystery of his will, according to the purpose he displayed in Christ as a plan for the fullness of time—to bring all things together in Christ, things in the heavens and things on earth. (Eph 1:8–10)

What is the Good News?

The Good News is that God has sent his Son Jesus Christ to redeem us, as promised to Abraham and his descendants. (422–424)

But when the fullness of time had come, God sent forth his Son, born of a woman . . . so we could be adopted as God's sons. (Gal 4:4–5)

How is it that we believe in Jesus Christ?

God the Father has chosen us, and his Holy Spirit has moved our hearts to believe that Jesus Christ is the Son of God and our Savior. (424)

Simon Peter replied, "You are the Messiah, the Son of the Living God!" (Mt 16:16)

What does the name "Jesus" mean?

In Hebrew "Jesus" means "God saves." At the Annunciation the Angel Gabriel gave Jesus this name, which summarizes his identity and mission. (430–435)

Salvation comes from no one else, for no other name under heaven has been given to us by which we may be saved. (Acts 4:12)

What does the title "Christ" mean?

"Christ" is a Greek word derived from the Hebrew *messiah*, which means "anointed." In order to fulfill his unique mission, Jesus was anointed as priest, prophet, and king. (436–440)

So let the whole house of Israel know beyond any doubt—this Jesus whom you crucified God made both Lord and Messiah. (Acts 2:36)

What does the title "Lord" mean?

The title "Lord" is derived from the Greek *kyrios*, which Christian scribes used to translate the Hebrew name for God, *YHWH*. (446–451, 455)

No one can say, "Jesus is Lord!" except under the influence of the Holy Spirit. (1 Cor 12:3)

What does the title "Son of God" mean?

When used to describe Jesus Christ, the title "Son of God" acknowledges his divine Sonship. It is not used in the common biblical sense of adoptive sonship nor of intimate relationship as in the case of angels, the Israelites, or their kings, but to declare the fact that Jesus Christ is truly the God-Man. (441–445, 454)

And we saw his glory, glory as of the only begotten of the Father. (Jn 1:14)

Why did the Son of God become a man?

The Son of God became a man to teach us what to believe, to show us the right way to live, and above all to die and rise for our salvation. Jesus came to (461):
- ❖ reconcile us to God in order to save us (457);
- ❖ manifest God's love to us (458);
- ❖ offer us himself as the model of holiness (459);
- ❖ make us sharers in his divine nature (460).

In these last days he [God] has spoken to us through a Son.... (Heb 1:2)

What is the Incarnation?

The Incarnation means that God the Son, the Second Person of the Blessed Trinity, took to himself a human nature and became a true man—Jesus of Nazareth. (461–463)

And the Word became flesh and dwelt among us. (Jn 1:14)

Is Jesus truly God and truly man?

Jesus is truly God and truly man. (464)

We know that the Son of God has come and has given us under-standing so that we can know the One who is true, and we are in the true One, in his Son Jesus Christ. He is the true God and ever-lasting life. (1 Jn 5:20)

What can we understand about Jesus's being both God and man?

Jesus is only one Person, and that Person is God the Son. Because he has two natures—the divine nature and a human nature—he is both God and man. This mystery is called the hypostatic union. (252, 464–469)

No one has ever seen God; the only begotten Son of God, who is in the bosom of the Father he has revealed him. (Jn 1:18)

What do we mean by nature and person?

Nature is *what* something or someone is; *person* is *who* someone is. Jesus is one Person with two natures. This is a great mystery of our faith. (467)

Is Jesus still both God and man?

Yes, Jesus is still both God and man and will continue to be so forever.

How is the Son of God man?

The Son of God assumed a human nature. This means that everything Christ is and does expresses his divinity through his human intellect, will, and body. (470)

Have I been with you so long and yet you do not recognize me, Philip? Whoever has seen me has seen the Father! How can you say, "Show us the Father"? Don't you believe that I am in the Father and the Father is in me? (Jn 14:9–10)

If he was God, why do we say that Jesus did the Father's will?

Jesus possesses two natures and all their operations. The human and divine natures are in total agreement because they belong to one Person, the Second Person of the Blessed Trinity. (475)

The Father who abides in me does his works. (Jn 14:10)

Was there a limit to Christ's human knowledge?

Yes, as man Christ's human knowledge was limited by the historical conditions surrounding him. However, he also had divine knowledge of the eternal plan of God and divine insight into the thoughts of other persons. (472–474)

If I told you about earthly things and you did not believe, how will you believe if I tell you about heavenly things? (Jn 3:12)

Do we venerate Christ's human body?

We certainly venerate Christ's human body and images of it because with it he expressed his divinity, and by his suffering and death he redeemed us. (476–477)

Since through the blood of Jesus we have the confidence to enter the sanctuary by the new and living way he opened for us through the curtain—that is, the way of his flesh—and since we have a great high priest who has charge over God's household, let us approach with true hearts and the full assurance of our faith. . . . (Heb 10:19–22)

How do we depict the human love of Christ for us?

Devotion to the Sacred Heart of Jesus illustrates the love Jesus had for his Father and for each of us. (478)

And this life I live now in the flesh, I live through faith in the Son of God, who loved me and gave himself up for me. (Gal 2:20)

How did God prepare the world for the coming of Christ?

Over the centuries, God gradually prepared the world for the coming of Christ, especially through the work of the prophets. His immediate forerunner was John the Baptist, who baptized Jesus with the baptism of repentance. During Advent the Church prepares for Christ's coming in the spirit of John the Baptist. (522–526)

> *You yourselves can bear witness to me that I said, "I am not the Messiah, but that I am the one sent before him." (Jn 3:28)*

Where do we learn about the life and teachings of Jesus?

We learn about the life and teachings of Jesus from the New Testament, especially the Gospels.

Why do the Gospels not provide more complete information about the life of Jesus?

The Gospels have the specific purpose of announcing that God has visited and redeemed his people in his Son Jesus Christ. The information it gives is sufficient for this purpose. (514)

> *Now there are also many other things that Jesus did; if every one of them were written down, I do not suppose the world itself would have room for the books that would be written. (Jn 21:25)*

What is the Annunciation?

The Annunciation is the day (usually celebrated March 25) on which the Church recalls the Angel Gabriel's announcement to Mary that she was to be the Mother of God, her acceptance, and the Incarnation of the Son of God by the power of the Holy Spirit. (484–486)

> *The angel said to her, "The Holy Spirit will come upon you, and the power of the Most High will overshadow you; therefore, the holy*

child to be born will be called Son of God." . . . Mary said, "Behold, the handmaid of the Lord; let it be done to me according to your word." (Lk 1:35, 38)

Is Mary really the Mother of God?

Yes, Mary is really the Mother of God, because Jesus, the son truly born of her, is also the eternal Son of God. Mary is called *Theotokos*, the Mother of God. (495)

"But how is it that the mother of my Lord should come to me?" (Lk 1:43)

What is the Immaculate Conception?

The Immaculate Conception means that Mary was conceived without original sin and endowed with grace. This special privilege was given to her because Christ would be born of her. In 1854 Pope Pius IX proclaimed the Immaculate Conception a dogma, and it is celebrated on December 8. (490–493)

[God] chose us in Christ before the foundation of the world to be holy and blameless before him. (Eph 1:4)

What is the virgin birth?

The virgin birth means that Mary remained a virgin before, during, and after the birth of Christ. (496–501)

Mary said to the angel, "How will this come about, since I do not know man?" (Lk 1:34)

Why do the Gospels refer to "brothers and sisters" of the Lord?

When the Gospels speak of brothers and sisters of Jesus, the reference is to close relatives such as cousins, or perhaps fellow citizens of his hometown. We can't verify their identity, but we know they cannot be Mary's children because she was perpetually a virgin. (500)

Look, your mother and brothers are outside asking for you. (Mk 3:32)

How is St. Joseph related to Jesus and Mary?

Joseph was the true spouse of Mary and the foster father of Jesus. Joseph was guardian of the Virgin and her Child, and provided for Jesus and cared for him as a father for his son. He also taught Jesus a trade and initiated him into the religion of his people. (497)

Is not this the carpenter's son? (Mt 13:55)

Where was Jesus born?

Jesus was born in Bethlehem of Judea, the small town in which King David was born.

Since Joseph was of the house and family of David, he went up from Nazareth in Galilee to Bethlehem of Judea, the city of David. . . . (Lk 2:4)

Why did Jesus come as an infant?

Christ came into our world as an infant, born in poverty, because to be truly human he had to experience our life from birth to death. In this he gave us an example of humility and love. (525–526)

Therefore, whoever humbles himself like this child. . . . is the greatest in the kingdom of heaven. (Mt 18:4)

What do we know of the infancy of Jesus?

Little is known of his infancy. The Gospels mention the following events:

(a) *Circumcision.* On the eighth day after his birth Jesus was circumcised. This rite incorporated him into the covenant and charged him with participation in Israel's worship. (527)

And when eight days had passed for his circumcision they gave him the name Jesus. (Lk 2:21)

(b) *Epiphany.* This indicates the universality of Jesus's mission and commemorates the visit of the wise men from the East. The liturgy links this manifestation of Jesus with his baptism by John and the wedding at Cana, where Jesus performed the first of his signs. (528)

When Jesus was born in Bethlehem of Judea in the days of King Herod, behold, Magi from the East arrived in Jerusalem asking, "Where is the newborn King of the Jews?" (Mt 2:1–2)

(c) *Presentation.* This was the day Jesus, the firstborn Son, was officially offered in the temple, accepted by God, and recognized as the Messiah, but also as a sign that would be rejected. (529)

When the day came for their purification according to the Torah of Moses they took the child up to Jerusalem to present him to the Lord. (Lk 2:22)

(d) *Flight into Egypt.* The Holy Family sought refuge in Egypt to escape the murderous intention of King Herod. This event commemorates the slaughter of many innocent boys in Bethlehem and is a sign of Jesus's persecuted life. (530)

He came to his own home, yet his own people did not receive him. (Jn 1:11)

What was the outstanding characteristic of Jesus in his youth?

Jesus was outstanding for his obedience to God and to his parents. This virtue continued to be the hallmark of his life, especially evident in the passion. (531–534)

Then he went down with them and went to Nazareth, and he was subject to them. (Lk 2:51)

Did Jesus show us how to live?

Jesus showed us how to live especially by his example, that is, by the way he lived his private and public life. Although we know very little about his private life, he spent his public life teaching. It probably lasted shortly over two years, and it ended with his death and resurrection. (512–570)

Who, though he was in the form of God, did not consider equality with God something to hold on to. Instead, he emptied himself and took on the form of a slave, born in human likeness, and to all appearances a man. He humbled himself and became obedient, even unto death, death on a cross. (Phil 2:6–8)

Do the Gospels show that Jesus is truly God?

Yes, the Gospels show that Jesus is truly God. In ways that were very clear for the people of his time and country, Jesus showed that he was God. (515) For example, Jesus said:

All things have been given to me by my Father, and no one knows the Son except the Father, nor does anyone know the Father except the Son, and whoever the Son chooses to reveal him to. (Mt 11:27)

How did Jesus back up his claim to be God?

Jesus backed up his claim to be God by working miracles and prophesying. (515)

For the works the Father has given me to bring to completion, the very works I do, bear witness to me that the Father sent me, and the Father who sent me, he has borne witness to me. (Jn 5:36–37)

What is a miracle?

A miracle is something that takes place outside of the ordinary working of nature's laws. This is something only God can do, either directly or through human instruments. (547–550)

[Jesus] called out with a loud voice, "Lazarus, come out!" The dead man came out with his hands and feet bound with thongs and his face wrapped with a cloth. (Jn 11:43–44)

What was the greatest miracle of Jesus?

His greatest miracle was his resurrection. (648)

I have power to lay it [my body] down and I have power to take it up again. (Jn 10:18)

What is prophecy?

Prophecy may be concerned with future events, but it is basically the mediation and interpretation of the divine mind and will through past and present events. (64, 436)

And when I am lifted up from the earth I will draw all men to myself. (Jn 12:32)

What were some events Jesus prophesied?

Jesus prophesied his passion and resurrection, his denial by Peter, his betrayal by Judas, and the destruction of the temple (which took place about forty years after his ascension). (557–558, 585)

I say to you, not a stone here will be left upon a stone which will not be torn down. (Mt 24:2)

Why do the miracles and prophecies of Jesus prove that he is divine?

The miracles and prophecies of Jesus could only have been done if God was with him and thus approved what he had said about being divine. (547–548)

The very works I do, bear witness to me that the Father sent me. (Jn 5:36)

Jesus was called master or teacher. Whom did he teach?

Jesus taught everyone who came to listen to him, but he gave special training to his disciples, especially the twelve apostles. In the Gospels and through the Church, Jesus continues to be our teacher. (427, 541–546)

He spoke to the people only in parables and explained everything to his own disciples in private. (Mk 4:34)

Those who followed Jesus in a special way were called disciples or apostles. What do these words mean?

Disciple means "learner" or "follower"; *apostle* means one "who is sent." Jesus had been sent into the world by his Father; now he was preparing to send his apostles into the world as his messengers. (520, 858, 1506)

Then he went up the mountain and called those he wanted, and they came to him. He chose twelve, whom he also called apostles, to stay with him and to send them out to preach. (Mk 3:13–14)

What is the redemption?

The redemption refers to God's saving work through Jesus, who laid down his life that we might be freed of sin and reconciled to the Father. (601–602)

For even the Son of Man came, not to be served, but to serve, and to give his life as a ransom for many. (Mk 10:45)

Why did Jesus die?

Jesus died to deliver us from sin, both the sin of our first parents and our personal sins. By his death Jesus reconciled us to the Father so that we might receive God's life called grace and reach eternal salvation. (601–615)

Through one man's obedience many will be made righteous . . . so that just as sin reigned in death so too would grace reign in

reconciliation leading to eternal life through our Lord Jesus Christ.
(Rom 5:19, 21)

Did Jesus have to suffer and die to save us?

Jesus did not have to suffer and die to save us, but he freely chose to do so. (606, 609)

I am the good shepherd; the good shepherd lays down his life for his sheep. No one takes it from me; on the contrary, I lay it down on my own. (Jn 10:11, 18)

What do we learn from Jesus's offering of his life for our sake?

The death of Jesus teaches us how much he loves us and how evil sin is. (604)

Greater love than this no man has—to lay down his life for his friends. (Jn 15:13)

Did God have to redeem us?

God freely chose to redeem us out of his great love. We did not merit this; it was a free gift of God. (604–605)

The proof of God's love for us is that Christ died for us while we were still sinners. (Rom 5:8)

Who is responsible for the death of Jesus?

All of us are responsible for his death because of our sinfulness; we cannot put the blame on particular individuals or groups. (597–598)

. . . Jesus would die for the nation, and not only for the nation but also so that the scattered children of God might gather into one. (Jn 11:51–52)

Did Jesus die for all people?

As the Redeemer of the human race, Jesus died for all people without exception. (605)

He is the expiation for our sins, and not only for ours but for the sins of the whole world. (1 Jn 2:2)

Did Jesus really die?

Jesus really did die. This means that his human soul separated from his human body. To remove any doubt, the Gospels tell us clearly that when the soldier pierced Jesus's heart with a lance he was already dead (see Jn 19:33–34). (626)

Christ died for our sins in accordance with the Scriptures. (1 Cor 15:3)

What do we call the sufferings of Jesus before his death?

The sufferings of Jesus before his death are called his passion. (610)

What is Good Friday?

Good Friday is the Friday before Easter, on which day we remember in a special way our Savior's sufferings and death for us on Calvary.

Why do we say that Jesus descended into hell?

"Hell" here refers to the abode of the just who died before the coming of Jesus. After his death, Jesus descended there in his soul to free those who had been awaiting deliverance. (631–635)

The hour is coming, and is now, when the dead will hear the voice of the Son of God, and those who listen to it will live. (Jn 5:25)

Did Jesus truly rise to life again?

The Gospels clearly tell us that Jesus did truly rise to life again. The reuniting of Jesus's body and soul, called the resurrection, was brought about by God's power, which the Father, Son, and Holy Spirit each possess. (639)

Why are you looking for he who lives among the dead? He is not here—he is risen. (Lk 24:5–6)

What was the new life of the resurrected Christ?

At the resurrection the same Jesus who had died came back to life, but in a glorious and empowered state, never to die again. Jesus's new life was that of heaven, no longer bound to the limits of time and space. (645–647)

After this he appeared in a different form to two of them as they were walking into the countryside. . . . (Mk 16:12)

Why is the resurrection of Jesus important?

The resurrection of Jesus shows that he truly is God as he said and, therefore, that his death really saved us. (651–655)

And if Christ was not raised then everything we proclaimed is in vain, and so is your faith. . . . As it is, Christ was raised from the dead. . . . (1 Cor 15:14, 20)

What does the resurrection of Jesus tell us about our future resurrection?

The resurrection of Jesus shows us what our resurrection will be like at the end of the world. Just as God's power united the body and soul of Jesus, so will our own bodies and souls be reunited by God's power at the end of time. (655)

Just as in Adam all men die, so too in Christ they will also come to life again. (1 Cor 15:22)

What followed the resurrection of Jesus?

After his resurrection, Jesus appeared to his followers several times to show that he had truly risen and to prepare them for their mission. Then he ascended to his Father. (659)

He also provided them with many proofs that he was still alive after his sufferings. . . . (Acts 1:3)

What is the visible departure of Jesus from this world called?

The visible departure of Jesus from this world is called the ascension. This important event is commemorated each year on the feast of the Ascension. (660)

I am ascending to my Father and your Father, and to my God and your God. (Jn 20:17)

What do we call the passion, death, resurrection, and ascension of Jesus?

The passion, death, resurrection, and ascension of Jesus are called the Paschal Mystery. "Paschal" refers to Passover and Easter; "mystery" here means event. (571)

How is Jesus present in our world today?

The risen and glorified Jesus "dwells on earth in his Church" (669). He is completely present (as both God and man) in the Eucharist. He is also present in the other sacraments, his actions that give us the Holy Spirit and grace. Also, by his power as God, he speaks to us through the Bible and the Church, especially the Pope.

I will be with you all the days until the end of the age. (Mt 28:20)

When will Christ come again?

Christ is the Lord of history and head of the Church, yet not all the earth is subject to him. At a future time known only to God, Christ will return in glory to fully establish his kingdom. (671–672)

"Lord, is this when you will restore the kingdom to Israel?" But he told them, "It is not for you to know the dates and times my Father has decided upon from his own authority." (Acts 1:6–7)

What is the last judgment?

The last judgment will be the day of God's justice and mercy when good will finally triumph over evil. The heart of each person who ever lived will be revealed. We will receive eternal reward or eternal punishment according to our works and our acceptance of God's grace. (678–679)

[The Son of Man] will sit on the throne of his glory, and all the nations will be gathered before him, and he will separate them from each other.... (Mt 25:31–32)

Belief in the Holy Spirit

Who is the Holy Spirit?

The Holy Spirit is the Third Person of the Blessed Trinity. (685)

In Christ you who heard the word of truth.. and believed it were sealed by the promised Holy Spirit. (Eph 1:13) (See also Rom 8:14, 17; Acts 1:8.)

Is the Holy Spirit God?

The Holy Spirit is God, as are the Father and the Son. (691)

The grace of the Lord Jesus Christ, the love of God, and the fellowship of the Holy Spirit be with you all. (2 Cor 13:13)

What are some other names for the Holy Spirit?

The Holy Spirit is also called Paraclete, Spirit of God, Gift of God, Spirit of Truth, Spirit of Adoption, and Giver of Life. (691–693)

But when he comes—the Spirit of truth—he will lead you to the whole truth. (Jn 16:13)

What does "paraclete" mean?

Paraclete means "someone called upon for help" (advocate, intercessor). The term also means "consoler." (692)

And I will ask the Father and he will give you another Intercessor to be with you forever. (Jn 14:16)

What does the Holy Spirit do for us?

The Holy Spirit transforms us through sanctifying grace, the virtues, his gifts, and actual graces. He helps us to know Jesus, our Savior, and our Father in heaven; the Spirit also helps us to pray and to evangelize. (733–736)

If we live in the Spirit, let us also follow the Spirit. (Gal 5:25)

What does the Holy Spirit do for the Church?

The Holy Spirit unites God's people, the Church, in faith and love, and gives us the grace Jesus won for us by his death on the cross. The Spirit guides the Church's chief teachers, the Pope and bishops united with him, so that they will faithfully hand on the truth Christ taught. (737)

So the church was at peace . . . ; it was being built up and proceeded in the fear of the Lord and it grew in numbers with the encouragement of the Holy Spirit. (Acts 9:31)

When did the Holy Spirit first make himself known to the followers of Jesus?

Although the Holy Spirit was active in the world before Jesus's resurrection, on Pentecost the Spirit descended on the disciples of Jesus with great power. The Spirit gave the apostles courage, a spirit of sacrifice, and a deeper understanding of the teachings of Jesus. The Spirit strengthened them with grace and united them more closely. (739–741)

Tongues as if of fire appeared to them, parting and coming to rest on each of them, and they were all filled with the Holy Spirit and began to speak in different tongues according to how the Spirit inspired them to speak. (Acts 2:3–4)

What special gift does the Holy Spirit give us?

The Holy Spirit gives us grace, a participation in the life of God, which Jesus won for us by his death on the cross. (1996–1997)

He has bestowed on us the great and precious promises so that through them you . . . may come to share in the divine nature. (2 Pt 1:4)

Belief in the Holy Catholic Church

The Mystery of the Church

What do we call the Church founded by Jesus?

We call the Church founded by Jesus the Catholic Church.

What is the Catholic Church?

The Catholic Church is the true Church founded by Jesus Christ, whose members are joined by bonds of spiritual communion: loyalty to the Pope and bishops joined with him, oneness in the truths to be believed and the moral code to be followed, and oneness in worship. The Church is a mystery, the sacrament of salvation, and the People of God journeying together toward eternal life. (771–776)

Why did Jesus start his Church?

Jesus started his Church to continue his mission of bringing all people to eternal salvation. (763) St. Peter told the first Christians:

You are a chosen race, a royal priesthood, a holy nation, a people set apart by God to proclaim his saving deeds, who called you out of darkness into his marvelous light. (1 Pt 2:9)

What special role does the Holy Spirit have in the life of the Church?

The Holy Spirit's special role in the Church is to keep the members faithful to the teachings of Jesus until the end of time. The Holy Spirit also helps the Church to constantly become holier. As the soul of the Church, the Holy Spirit inspires fearless preaching of the Gospel. (737, 767–768, 788, 797)

> . . . *The household of God, which is the Church of the living God, the pillar and foundation of the truth.* (1 Tm 3:15)

What is the Catholic faith?

The Catholic faith comprises the teachings of the Catholic Church, that which we believe—that which is universally believed.

Are all faiths equally true?

While all faiths in some way reflect the truth and goodness of God, only one can be the true faith. The fullness of Jesus's revelation—the truths to be believed, the way of life, the gifts of grace—subsists (is totally present) in the Catholic Church. (816, 830)

> *He has put all things under his feet and has given him as head over all things to the Church, which is his body, the fullness of the One who fills all things in their totality.* (Eph 1:22–23)

Is the Church both visible and spiritual?

The Church is both human and divine, a visible society which can be known through its structures, and a divine reality sustained by God. (771)

Who are the People of God?

Vatican II favored the biblical term "People of God" to designate the followers of Jesus Christ. These are all the baptized members of the Church. Catholics are fully incorporated into Christ's Church through grace, the sacraments, profession of the faith, and union with the Church's bishops united to the

Pope. However, Catholics who live in a state of serious sin have only an imperfect communion with the Church. Other baptized Christians, although not fully united to the Catholic Church, have a certain communion with it through the grace of Baptism. (781–786, 836–838)

> But you are a chosen race, a royal priesthood, a holy nation, a people set apart by God to proclaim his saving deeds. (1 Pt 2:9)

Why is the Church called Christ's Mystical Body?

The term "Mystical Body" refers to the real union of the Church's members (living and deceased) with Jesus, who is the Head, and with one another through the grace-giving activity of the Holy Spirit. (787–795)

> For just as we have many members in one body . . . in the same way we, many as we are, are one body in Christ, and each one of us is a part of the other. (Rom 12:4–5) (See also 1 Cor 12:27; Jn 15:4–5.)

What are the four characteristics by which we identify the true Church in our world today?

The true Church founded by Christ is one, holy, catholic (or universal), and apostolic. Only the Roman Catholic Church has these four characteristics or marks. (811–812)

How is the Catholic Church one?

Rooted in the mystery of the Trinity, the Church's unity consists especially in the bond of charity. It becomes visible in profession of the same faith, common worship, and union with the Church's pastors. (813–822)

> There is one Body and one Spirit, just as you were called to the one hope of your calling. One Lord, one faith, one baptism, one God and Father of us all, who is above all, through all, and in all. (Eph 4:4–6)

How is the Catholic Church holy?

Christ gave his life to make the Church holy and sent the Spirit to breathe holiness into it. Since all the Church's members are called to holiness, Christ gave the Church the means to help them toward this goal, especially the sacraments. (823–829)

> *In him the whole building is joined together and grows into a holy Temple in the Lord, and in him you are being built together into God's dwelling place in the Spirit.* (Eph 2:21–22)

How is the Catholic Church catholic or universal?

The Catholic Church is catholic or universal in two senses: first, because it contains the fullness of Christ in the means for salvation: doctrine, sacraments, and apostolic ministry; and second, because it is meant for all people of all places. (830–835)

> *Go, therefore, and make disciples of all nations, baptizing them in the name of the Father and of the Son and of the Holy Spirit, and teach them to observe all that I have commanded you and, behold, I will be with you all the days until the end of the age.* (Mt 28:19–20)

How is the Catholic Church apostolic?

The Church is apostolic because it is founded on the apostles, whose teaching the Church faithfully hands on. In this it is guided by its pastors, the bishops, who have succeeded to the pastoral office of the apostles. (857–865)

> *You were built upon a foundation of apostles and prophets, and Christ Jesus was its cornerstone.* (Eph 2:20)

Is the Catholic Church necessary for salvation?

The Catholic Church is necessary for salvation because Christ wills to give us the grace of salvation through his

Church. In some way this grace reaches even those who are not members of the Church. If through no fault of their own they do not know our Savior Jesus Christ and his Church, they can be saved if they seek God sincerely and try to live good lives. (846–848)

In Christ we have free and confident access to God through our faith in him. (Eph 3:12)

Christ's Faithful: Hierarchy, Laity, Consecrated Life

What is the Pope's role in the Church?

The Pope is the Vicar of Christ and the chief teacher and leader of God's people; he holds the place of Jesus in the Church. The Catholic Church will always have a pope because this is what Jesus wanted. (880, 882)

And now I tell you, that you are Peter, and on this rock I will build my Church. (Mt 16:18) (See also Jn 21:17.)

What is the primacy of the Pope?

The primacy of the Pope means the "first place" that the Pope holds in the Church in teaching, governing, and guiding Catholics in what they believe and in how they live. (881)

And he chose twelve of them, whom he also called apostles—Simon, whom he also named Peter. . . . (Lk 6:13–14)

What does the title "Prince of the Apostles" mean?

The title "Prince of the Apostles" was given to St. Peter, the first Pope. It means that he is the first among the apostles, the leader of the group. (883)

The Lord has really risen and has been seen by Simon. (Lk 24:34)

Why is it important to follow the Pope?

The Holy Spirit guides the Pope in teaching what to believe and do in order to be saved. In following him, we are assured of being on the right path. (798)

What is the Catholic Church's gift of infallibility?

The gift of infallibility is freedom from error when teaching a truth of faith or right living. It comes from the Holy Spirit and is given to the Pope when he teaches officially as head of the Church. It also pertains to the bishops united with him either in general council or when they express the teachings of the Church. (891–892)

> *Blessed are you, Simon bar Jonah, for it was not flesh and blood that revealed this to you, but my Father in heaven.* (Mt 16:17)

What does the term *ex cathedra* mean?

The Latin term *ex cathedra* means "from the chair" of St. Peter. It refers to the Pope's infallible statements regarding what Catholics must believe and live. (891, note 418)

What is Vatican City?

Vatican City is the city (which is also an independent nation) where the Pope lives. It consists of 108.7 acres situated within Rome, Italy. It contains the Pope's residence, St. Peter's Basilica, and the headquarters of various Church officials.

What is an encyclical?

An encyclical is a letter written by the Pope, often directed to the bishops, but intended for the whole Church and sometimes for all people.

What is the college of bishops?

The college of bishops refers to all the bishops throughout the world united with the Pope. They form one body called the hierarchy or apostolic college, which continues the apostolic college of St. Peter and the other apostles. (880)

When day came he called his disciples to him and he chose twelve of them, whom he also called apostles. . . . (Lk 6:13)

Who is a cardinal?

A cardinal is a high-ranking Church official appointed by the Pope to the college of cardinals (all the cardinals as a united body). Cardinals act as the Pope's advisors and can vote in a papal election. Today the cardinalate is conferred only on members of the clergy, generally bishops.

What is the role of bishops in the Church?

As authentic teachers of the faith handed down from the apostles, the bishops' primary task is to preach the Gospel. They also lead their people to holiness through the ministry of the sacraments. As pastors, bishops exercise the pastoral office of leadership and authority as servants of the flock. These three roles correspond to Christ's mission as prophet, priest, and king. (888–896)

Who are the hierarchy?

The hierarchy are the Church's authorities—especially the Pope and bishops, but also priests and deacons. Christ has entrusted them with the office of teaching, sanctifying, and governing the Church in his name and by his power. (873)

Follow me, and I will make you fishers of men. (Mt 4:19)

What is the magisterium?

The magisterium is the living teaching office of the Church, whose authority is exercised in the name of Jesus Christ. The Pope and the bishops teaching in communion with him authentically interpret the word of God, whether written or handed down, guarding and explaining it faithfully under the guidance of the Holy Spirit. (2032–2034)

> *All authority in heaven and on earth has been given to me. Go, therefore, and make disciples of all nations, baptizing them in the name of the Father and of the Son and of the Holy Spirit, and teach them to observe all that I have commanded you and, behold, I will be with you all the days until the end of the age.* (Mt 28:18–20)

What form does the magisterium take?

It takes two forms:
- ❖ the extraordinary magisterium, which consists of dogmatic definitions. These do not add anything to divine revelation, but give it a new clarity. We adhere to these teachings with the obedience of faith.
- ❖ the ordinary magisterium, which consists of the daily teachings of the Pope and the bishops in communion with him. We respond to these teachings with religious assent.

What is an ecumenical council?

An ecumenical or universal council is a meeting of the bishops of the whole world, called together by the Pope to discuss and explain Church teaching and to set forth guidelines for the People of God. An ecumenical council's conclusions must be approved by the Pope. (884)

Who is an archbishop?

An archbishop is usually the bishop of a large diocese (archdiocese), who oversees neighboring dioceses.

What is an archdiocese or diocese?

An archdiocese or diocese is a territory made up of parishes placed by the Pope under the care of a Church leader called a bishop or archbishop.

What is a parish?

A parish is a community of Christians who worship together in the same church and are led by the same priest, usually called a pastor, and his assistants. (2179)

Who is the pastor?

The pastor is the priest in charge of a parish and its spiritual leader or shepherd.

Who is the vicar general?

The vicar general is an auxiliary bishop or priest appointed to help in the government of a diocese. He shares in the bishop's jurisdiction.

What is a chancery office of an archdiocese or diocese?

A chancery office is the headquarters of a diocese or archdiocese, where Church transactions are carried out and recorded.

What is canon law?

Canon law is the official compilation of Church law which is found in the *Code of Canon Law*. Based on Gratian's Decree of 1140, canon law was promulgated (formally proclaimed) in

1917 by Pope Benedict XV. In 1983 Pope John Paul II promulgated the new *Code of Canon Law*.

What is an *imprimatur*?

An *imprimatur* is the bishop's permission to publish writings about faith or morals, and indicates the work is free from doctrinal or moral error. Canon law specifies the types of books that require an *imprimatur*.

Who are the laity?

The laity are all the faithful except those in Holy Orders or who are members of a religious congregation. The laity share in the priestly, prophetic, and kingly office of Christ. (897–898)

> *Like living stones let yourselves be built up into a spiritual house.*
> (1 Pt 2:5)

What is the laity's role in the Church?

The laity exercise an indispensable role in the Church. They bring Christian witness into the social, political, and economic realms where they live and work. (898–912)

How do the laity participate in Christ's priestly office?

Through their lives, daily work, prayers, and all other activities, the laity offer spiritual sacrifices to God through Jesus Christ. In a special way parents share in the Church's mission through the Christian upbringing of their children. (901–903)

How do the laity participate in Christ's office of teaching?

The laity have a vital part to play in the Church's evangelizing mission. They do this through Christian witness, telling others about Jesus Christ, teaching, and using the communications media, according to their various circumstances. (904–907)

How do the laity participate in Christ's pastoral office?

The laity can bring Gospel values into the economic and political spheres and work for a more just society. They can also serve in various pastoral ministries in the Church, and on pastoral councils, diocesan synods, etc. (908–913)

Who are the Eastern Rite Catholics?

The Eastern Rite Catholics are fully Catholic—united to the Pope in the unity of faith. They differ slightly from Western (Latin Rite) Catholics in the way they celebrate Mass and the sacraments, as well as in various Church laws and customs. These rites are honored because of their ancient origins. (1203)

Who are the Eastern Orthodox Christians?

The Eastern Orthodox are members of ancient Churches established in the East (primarily Eastern and Southeastern Europe and Western Asia). Due to various difficulties, the Eastern Orthodox and Latin Churches finally split during the Middle Ages. The Orthodox have the Mass and the seven sacraments but do not accept the authority of the Pope. (838)

What is ecumenism?

Ecumenism is the effort of Christians to study and pray together in the hope of becoming one united Church. It is also called the ecumenical movement. (820–822)

> But I am praying not only for them but also for those who believe in me through their word, so that all may be one, just as you, Father, are in me and I in you. (Jn 17:20–21)

What is the Church's mission?

The Church's mission is to preach the Gospel to all people throughout the world. The term "missions" is often used to designate those places where people have not yet heard the Gospel. But a major challenge for the Church today is to re-evangelize in countries that were formerly Christian. (850)

Such a life is good and acceptable in the sight of God our Savior, whose wish is that all may be saved and may come to knowledge of the truth. (1 Tm 2:3–4)

Who is a missionary?

A missionary is a person dedicated to spreading God's word (evangelizing), especially in those areas of the world that are not predominantly Christian. (849)

Go, therefore, and make disciples of all nations. (Mt 28:19)

What is evangelization?

Evangelization is spreading the Gospel—the Good News about what Jesus has done for us, what he expects of us, and what he promises us. Jesus says to us:

I am the light of the world. (Jn 8:12)

You are the light of the world. (Mt 5:14)

Go into the whole world and proclaim the Good News to all creation. (Mk 16:15)

Why did Jesus call us the "light of the world"?

Jesus called us the "light of the world" because he wants us to lead good lives and help others come to know him. (2044–2046)

Grow in the grace and knowledge of our Lord and Savior Jesus Christ. (2 Pt 3:18)

How can we help the missions?

We can help the missions by prayer, contributions, and sacrifices, or by volunteering to help with a missionary project.

What is consecrated life?

Consecrated life is a way of life followed by those who dedicate themselves totally to Jesus Christ by following the evangelical counsels of poverty, chastity, and obedience. "It is the *profession* of these counsels, within a permanent state of life recognized by the Church, that characterizes the life consecrated to God." (915) There are different forms of consecrated life.

What is religious life?

Religious life is a special way of following Jesus. Religious are persons who make the vows of chastity, obedience, and poverty in a religious community. (925–927)

What is the origin of religious life?

Religious life is rooted in Sacred Scripture, especially in the words and examples of Jesus, the Divine Master.

> *Amen, I say to you, there is no one who has left his house or wife or brothers or parents or children for the sake of the kingdom of God who will not receive many times more in this time, and in the coming age, life eternal.* (Lk 18:29–30)

What is the purpose of the religious vows?

Religious vows are meant to free the mind and heart of the religious so that he or she can love God entirely and serve his people with wholehearted devotion. This life is like a foretaste of the way we will live in heaven. (916)

Is religious life a sacrament?

Religious life is not a sacrament. Religious publicly profess the three vows of poverty, chastity, and obedience in imitation of Jesus. They also promise to serve the Church through the particular apostolic work of their congregation. Although they do not receive a specific sacrament for this, religious are to be signs and servants of the kingdom for the rest of the faithful. (916)

What does religious chastity mean?

Religious chastity is the vow by which religious freely dedicate their whole lives to God, foregoing marriage and family life.

The unmarried man concerns himself with the Lord's affairs, with how to please the Lord. (1 Cor 7:32)

What does religious poverty mean?

Religious poverty is the vow by which religious give up the ownership of material goods and share things in common, so that they will find their "treasure" in heaven.

If you want to be perfect, go sell your possessions and give to the poor and you will have treasure in heaven, and come follow me. (Mt 19:21)

What does religious obedience mean?

Religious obedience is the vow by which religious pledge to obey the rule of their religious congregation and their superiors who represent God for them. They do this in imitation of the obedience of Jesus to his Father's will.

My food is to do the will of the one who sent me, and to bring his work to completion. (Jn 4:34)

Who is a consecrated virgin?

A consecrated virgin is a Christian woman who commits herself to a life of virginity and service through the diocesan bishop. Consecrated virgins dedicate their lives to God but do not live in a religious community. (922–924)

Who is a hermit?

A hermit is a person devoted totally to God in solitude, silence, prayer, and penance. The life of a hermit is one of surrender to the mystery of God, personal intimacy with Christ, and "silent preaching." (920–921)

What are secular institutes?

Secular institutes are institutes of consecrated life whose members do not live in community. They commit themselves to live the evangelical counsels and to perform works of evangelization and charity, acting as true "leaven" within society. (928–929)

What are societies of apostolic life?

Societies of apostolic life are congregations in which religious vows may or may not be taken, but the members live as brothers or sisters, observing a rule of life, living a common life, and performing a common apostolate. (930)

What is the communion of saints?

The communion of saints is the communication of spiritual help among the members of Christ's body (the Church) in heaven, on earth, and in purgatory. (946)

> *Whether we live or whether we die we belong to the Lord. This is why Christ died and came to life—so he would be Lord of both the dead and the living.* (Rom 14:8–9)

What is a saint?

A saint is a person who lives a holy and virtuous life. The name is generally applied to a "canonized" saint, that is, a person whose holiness the Church has solemnly recognized. (825, 828)

Offer your whole lives as a living sacrifice which will be holy and pleasing to God—this is your spiritual worship. (Rom 12:1)

What is a patron saint?

A patron saint is a special person to imitate and pray to for help, a heavenly protector, often one's name saint. Typically a patron saint is regarded as the intercessor and advocate in heaven of a nation, place, craft, activity, class, clan, family, or person. (2156)

I pray you, let me inherit a double share of your spirit. (2 Kgs 2:9)

What is a martyr?

A martyr is a person who allows himself or herself to be put to death rather than to deny the Christian faith. (2473–2474)

As he was being stoned Stephen cried out and said, "Lord Jesus, receive my spirit!" (Acts 7:59)

What is excommunication?

Excommunication is a penalty specified in canon law for certain grave offenses. It means that the person is separated from communion with the Church and cannot receive the sacraments. (1463)

What is schism?

Schism is a breaking away from the authority of the Pope and the unity (oneness) of the Church. (2089)

Let there be no divisions among you. Can Christ be divided? (1 Cor 1:10, 13)

Why is Mary called the Mother of the Church?

Mary plays a special role in God's plan of salvation because she was called to be the Mother of God. Closely united to Jesus, Mary is "the Church's model of faith and charity," and she is our spiritual mother. (963–970)

What can we learn from the history of the Church?

The history of the Church shows that Jesus is with his Church, as he promised, despite all persecution, and he has raised up saints in every period for God's people to imitate. Although its members have sinned and often made grave errors, the Church has preached the Gospel and tried to bring people to salvation.

Life Everlasting

What is death?

Death is the separation of soul and body, when the body of a human being becomes lifeless while the soul continues to live. (1005)

> *We would prefer to leave our bodies and be at home with the Lord.* (2 Cor 5:8)

What is a funeral?

For a Catholic, a funeral is the service for the deceased and the ceremonies connected with the burial of the dead. The central focus of the Catholic funeral liturgy is the funeral Mass. (1680–1690)

> *What is perishable when it is sown is imperishable when it is raised. A physical body is sown, a spiritual body is raised.* (1 Cor 15:42, 44)

What is a cemetery?

A cemetery is a place for burying the dead. For Catholics the burial ground or plot of land is to be consecrated or blessed.

What is cremation?

Cremation is the reduction of a human body to ashes by fire. The Church earnestly recommends that our ancient custom of burying the dead be observed. Cremation, however, is permitted unless it has been chosen for reasons which are contrary to the Christian teaching on the resurrection of the body. When cremation is chosen, the ashes or "cremains" must then be interred properly in a cemetery. Catholic burial practice calls for the cremains to be buried in an urn within a consecrated grave or placed inside a mausoleum. (2301)

What is the false belief called "reincarnation"?

Reincarnation is the erroneous concept that the souls of the dead return to earth in new forms or bodies. It is also called "transmigration of souls."

And the dust returns to the earth as it was, and the spirit returns to God who gave it. (Eccl 12:7)

What awaits a person after death and individual judgment?

After death and individual judgment a person may go to heaven for all eternity, or to purgatory temporarily and then to heaven, or to hell for all eternity. (1022)

Right now we see indistinctly, as in a mirror, but then we will see face to face. At present my knowledge is incomplete, but then I will truly understand, as God understands me. (1 Cor 13:12)

What does "eternal" mean?

"Eternal" means without beginning or end.

What is eternity?

In relation to God eternity means no beginning, end, or change. We speak of God's eternity, referring to his unending, unchanging Being. While we are not eternal, we will share in eternal life after death, life that lasts forever. For the just this life will be the complete and perfect happiness of heaven. (1020, 1023)

I am the resurrection and the life! Whoever believes in me, even if he should die, will live, and everyone who lives and believes in me shall never die. (Jn 11:25–26)

What is the particular judgment?

The particular judgment, also called the individual judgment, is Christ's judgment of a person immediately after death. (1021)

We always bear the death of Jesus in our bodies so the life of Jesus may also be revealed in our bodies. (2 Cor 4:10)

What is the beatific vision?

The beatific vision is the clear and immediate vision and experience of God enjoyed by the angels and saints in heaven. (163, 2548, 2550)

He took me in the spirit to a great high mountain and showed me the holy city Jerusalem coming down out of heaven from God with God's glory. The city had no need for the sun or the moon to shine on it, for God's glory illuminated the city and the Lamb was its lamp. (Rev 21:10–11, 23)

Who are the "blessed"?

The "blessed" are the souls of the dead who are in heaven. The title "blessed" is also given to a person who has been beatified or declared "blessed" by the Church. (1025, 1029)

Be faithful unto death, and I will give you the crown of life. (Rev 2:10)

Is there any pain or sorrow or sin in heaven?

In heaven there is no pain, sorrow, sin, or whatever could cause unhappiness. There cannot even be the threat or fear of these things.

Will we know our family and friends in heaven?

Yes, and we will rejoice with them in God.

Could life in heaven be boring?

Life in heaven could never be boring because we will always be finding out new and wonderful things about God.

Will everyone have the same degree of happiness in heaven?

In heaven everyone will be perfectly happy according to their capacity for happiness. This capacity will be greater for those who loved God more unselfishly on earth.

What is purgatory?

Purgatory is a condition of purification after death in which good souls who are imperfectly prepared for heaven are cleansed from the effects of their sins before they enter heaven. (1030–1032)

> *But whoever speaks against the Holy Spirit will not be forgiven, neither in this age nor in the age to come.* (Mt 12:32)

How long will purgatory last?

After the general judgment, there will no longer be a need for purification, since God's kingdom will have arrived in its fullness. (1031)

> *Then I saw a new heavens and a new earth—the first heavens and the first earth had passed away and the sea was no more.* (Rev 21:1)

Can we help the souls in purgatory?

We can help the souls in purgatory with our prayers, especially through the Mass, and by penance, acts of charity, and gaining indulgences for them. (1032)

Therefore he made atonement for the dead, so that they might be delivered from their sin. (2 Mc 12:45)

How long will heaven and hell last?

Heaven and hell will last forever. (1029, 1035)

There will no longer be night, and they will have no need for a lamp's light or for the light of the sun, for the Lord God will shine upon them and they will reign forever and ever. (Rev 22:5)

What is hell?

Hell is everlasting suffering and separation from God. (1033)

Get away from me, you cursed, into the eternal fire prepared for the Devil and his angels. . . . (Mt 25:41)

Who are the damned?

The damned are those who suffer everlasting punishment in hell because of their free and unrepented choice of mortal sin. (1034)

He is being patient with you because he does not want anyone to be destroyed—he wants everyone to come to repentance. But the day of the Lord will come like a thief. (2 Pt 3:9–10)

Is God cruel to make hell last forever?

God is not cruel, but just, to make hell last forever. The persons who will spend eternity in hell will have chosen to remain apart from God by the way they spent their earthly lives.

What is the pain of loss?

The pain of loss is one of the sufferings of those in hell or purgatory. It is awareness of being separated from our good and loving God. (1035)

What is the pain of sense?

The pain of sense refers to the other sufferings of hell or purgatory, a torment that is, or feels like, physical pain. (1034)

And whoever says, "You fool!" shall be liable to the fire of Gehenna. (Mt 5:22)

Can we help the souls in hell?

We cannot help the souls in hell, because their state is eternally and justly settled. (1033)

What is the second coming?

The second coming refers to Christ's return in glory at the end of the world, when he will reward the just and punish those who have persisted in doing evil. All the people who ever lived will be assembled for the general judgment, and the whole universe will be transformed as the kingdom of God is established. (1038–1041)

For the Son of Man will come in the glory of his Father with his angels, and then he will pay each according to their work. (Mt 16:27) (See also Mt 26:64; Acts 1:11.)

What is the general judgment?

The general or universal judgment, also known as the last judgment, will happen at the end of the world when God will make known everyone's eternal destiny in the presence of all humanity. (678–679, 1038–1041)

Because the hour is coming in which all those in the tombs will hear his voice, and they will come out, those who did good deeds to the resurrection of life, but those who wrought evil to the resurrection of judgment. (Jn 5:28–29)

Will our resurrected bodies be the same then as they are now?

Our resurrected bodies will be ours, but transformed. The bodies of the just will be in a glorified state, which means that they will no longer have physical needs and will be endowed with qualities that they did not possess in their mortal existence. (990)

The dead will be raised imperishable and we will be transformed. For this corruptible body must be clothed in incorruptibility, and this mortal body must be clothed in immortality. (1 Cor 15:52–53)

What is meant by the "glorified body"?

The glorified body is the body of one who has been raised from death to eternal life on the last day. No longer subject to suffering and death, our bodies will be transformed in glory. (999–1000)

Those who are wise shall shine like the brightness of the firmament; and those who turn many to righteousness, like the stars for ever and ever. (Dn 12:3)

Has the body of any human person been preserved from corruption and taken into heaven?

By a special privilege, the body of the Blessed Virgin Mary has been preserved from corruption and taken into heaven. On November 1, 1950, Pope Pius XII proclaimed Mary's Assumption a dogma of faith. This feast is celebrated on August 15. (966, 974)

What will happen at the end of the world?

At the end of the world the bodies of all people will rise from the earth to be reunited to their souls forever. The bodies of the just will share in the souls' glory; the bodies of the damned will share the punishment. (1042)

> *Many of those who sleep in the dust of the earth shall awake, some to everlasting life, and some to shame and everlasting contempt.* (Dn 12:2)

When will the end of the world occur?

We do not know when the world will end.

> *But as for that day and hour, no one knows—not the angels in heaven, nor the Son, but only the Father.* (Mt 24:36)

THE CELEBRATION OF THE
CHRISTIAN MYSTERY

The Liturgy

What is the liturgy?

The liturgy is the public work or service of God by which Christ continues the redemption through the Church. (1069)

> *May God . . . grant that you may live in harmony with one another in accordance with Christ Jesus, so that with one mind and one mouth you may glorify the God and Father of our Lord Jesus Christ.* (Rom 15:5–6)

What is the meaning of liturgy?

As with all of God's work, the liturgy is his blessing to us. Our response is adoration and thanksgiving. (1079)

What is the focus of the liturgy?

The saving life and mission of Christ is the central teaching of our faith; the Church's liturgy proclaims and celebrates this same mystery. (1067–1068)

> *To me, the least of all the saints, was given the grace of proclaiming to the Gentiles the unfathomable riches of Christ and to reveal for all the plan of the mystery that was hidden for ages in God, the creator of all things, so that the multi-faceted wisdom of God might now be made known through the church to the rulers and powers in the heavens, in accordance with the eternal plan he carried out in Christ Jesus our Lord.* (Eph 3:8–11)

How is the Trinity honored through the liturgy?

In the liturgy the Father is adored as Creator, the Son as our brother and Redeemer, the Holy Spirit as the giver of all gifts. (1077–1109)

What place does the Word of God have in the liturgy?

The Word of God speaks of the "wonders" worked in the sacraments and expresses our response of faith. Therefore, the Word of God has an integral role in each liturgical act. (1153–1155)

Receive instruction from his mouth, and lay up his words in your heart. (Job 22:22)

Do music and art have a place in liturgy?

Music and art have always been used to enhance liturgies by lending beauty to the celebration and by lifting hearts and minds to God. They are best used when they illustrate the Word of God. (1156–1162)

Let the Word of Christ dwell in you richly; teach and admonish each other with all wisdom; sing psalms, hymns, and spiritual songs to God with thanks in your hearts. (Col 3:16)

What is the Liturgy of the Hours?

The Liturgy of the Hours is the public and official common prayer of the Catholic Church. It is prayed daily by priests, religious, and an ever-increasing number of the laity. This form of the liturgy, based on the Psalms, is meant as a complement to Eucharistic devotion. (1174–1178)

Pray at all times in the Spirit with every manner of prayer and supplication. (Eph 6:18)

What is the liturgical year?

The liturgical year is the name given to the days and seasons within a year's time in which the Church celebrates

Christ's Paschal Mystery. The liturgical seasons are Advent, Christmas, Lent, Easter, and Ordinary Time. Sundays and holy days, feasts of Mary, celebrations of saints' days and other feast days light the Church year with warmth to stir the devotion of God's people. (1168–1173)

He has sent me . . . to proclaim the acceptable year of the Lord. (Lk 4:18–19)

What are liturgical colors?

Liturgical colors, usually green, purple, red, rose, and white, are colors of the priest's outer vestment, the chasuble. Each color helps to set the tone of joy, penance, etc., for particular liturgical seasons or feasts.

What is Advent?

"Advent" means coming. It is the short season, approximately four weeks, in which we prepare for Christmas and recall Christ's second coming at the end of time.

What is Christmas?

Christmas is the holy day of obligation on which we celebrate the birth of Jesus.

What is the Christmas season?

The Christmas season is the joyful period of time from Christmas to the celebration of the baptism of Jesus.

What is Lent?

Lent is the Church's forty-day season of preparation for Easter, in which Christians are expected to give more attention to prayer, penance, and good deeds.

What is Easter?

Easter Sunday is the Church's greatest day of celebration, when we rejoice over the resurrection of Jesus from the dead. (1169)

What is the Easter Season?

The Easter Season is the most joyous season of the Church's year—the fifty days from Easter to Pentecost.

What is the Easter Vigil?

The Easter Vigil is a celebration held at any time during the hours of darkness that precede the Easter sunrise. ("Vigil" means a night watch.) It consists of a service of light, a Liturgy of the Word, a Baptismal Liturgy, and the Liturgy of the Eucharist.

What is Pentecost?

Seven weeks after Easter we celebrate Pentecost Sunday, which commemorates the Holy Spirit's descent upon the apostles and disciples gathered in the upper room. Pentecost is considered the "birthday" of the Church. (1076)

What is Ordinary Time?

Ordinary Time is the season of the Church year outside of the Advent-Christmas and Lent-Easter seasons. One part of Ordinary Time falls between the Christmas season and Lent, and the other part falls between Pentecost and Advent.

The Sacraments: Actions of Jesus

What are the sacraments?

The sacraments are sacred signs through which Jesus gives us his Spirit and makes us holy and pleasing to him by grace. (1116, 1131)

All the people kept trying to touch him, because power kept coming out from him and healing them all. (Lk 6:19)

What is a sacramental sign?

A sacramental sign is something that we can hear or see, which tells us something about the sacrament we are about to receive. In every sacrament words make up part of the sign. (1145–1155)

What does "holy" mean?

Holy means "like God" or "close to God." It can also mean "set apart." God's holiness is the greatness and goodness that set him apart from all his creatures. Through the sacraments Jesus makes his people holy by grace. The Church, as well as its ceremonies, feasts, buildings, etc., are holy because they are of God. (1123)

He who called you is holy, and so you too should be holy in all your conduct, since it is written, "You shall be holy because I am holy." (1 Pt 1:15–16)

What is sacramental grace?

Sacramental grace is the particular grace of the Holy Spirit which each sacrament gives; for example, Confirmation strengthens our commitment to Christ. Through each sacrament the Holy Spirit transforms us and unites us to Christ. (1129)

We are sharing in God's work and we urge you not to accept God's grace in vain. (2 Cor 6:1)

Can we be sure Jesus acts through the sacraments?

Jesus always acts through the sacraments if we receive them under the proper conditions. The sacrament and its grace will benefit us also according to our dispositions or attitude—for example, the degree of our faith and love. (1127–1129, 1131)

His divine power has bestowed on us everything that pertains to life and holiness through our knowledge of the One who called us by his own glory and power. (2 Pt 1:3)

What role does the minister of the sacrament have?

The minister of the sacrament acts in the name of Christ and the Church and thus guarantees that Christ is truly at work in each sacrament. Although ordained ministers (bishop, priest, deacon) are the ordinary ministers of most sacraments, in marriage the man and woman minister the sacrament to each other. The priest or deacon is witness to the sacramental action of the spouses. The sacraments are to be celebrated according to the direction and intention of the Church in order to confer the power of the Lord. (1119–1120, 1128)

He said to them again, "Peace be with you! As the Father has sent me, I, too, send you." (Jn 20:21)

How many sacraments are there?

There are seven sacraments: Baptism, Confirmation, Eucharist, Penance, Anointing of the Sick, Holy Orders, and Matrimony. (1113, 1210)

If you knew the gift of God and who it is who is saying to you, "Give me a drink," you would have asked him and he would have given you living water. (Jn 4:10)

Who gave us the sacraments?

Jesus gave us the sacraments and continues to give each one of them. He does this through the Church, which is his Mystical Body. (1114, 1117, 1120)

Just as the living Father sent me, and I live because of the Father, so too, whoever feeds on me will live because of me. (Jn 6:57)

May the sacraments be divided into groups?

The sacraments may be divided into three groups. Baptism, Confirmation, and Eucharist are sacraments of initiation, or beginning in the Christian life. Penance and the Anointing of the Sick are sacraments of healing. Holy Orders and Matrimony are sacraments at the service of communion. (1211)

Why is the Church called a sacrament?

The Church is a sacrament—a "great sacrament" through which we receive the other seven. The Church is a sign that there is a God who cares about the world and that we are called to union with God and with one another. The seven sacraments, too, are signs of God's loving concern for people. (738, 774–776, 1118)

Like living stones let yourselves be built up into a spiritual house, a holy priesthood to offer spiritual sacrifices which are acceptable to God through Jesus Christ. (1 Pt 2:5)

Who celebrates the sacraments?

Sacraments are always celebrations of the whole community of Christ, of the Church universal, and the Church of heaven. For this reason, they are celebrated by the Church community, the priestly people, in which the ordained priesthood serves the baptismal priesthood by acting in the person of Christ. (1120, 1140–1141)

To the one . . . who made us a kingdom, priests to his God and Father—to him be glory and power forever, amen! (Rev 1:5–6)

Sacraments of Christian Initiation

Baptism

What is Baptism?

Baptism is the sacrament in which Jesus sends us his Spirit, who frees us from sin and gives us the grace by which we become God's children, heirs of heaven, members of the Church, and temples of the Blessed Trinity. (1213)

> *You were buried with him in baptism and in baptism you also rose with him through faith in the power of God, who raised Christ from the dead.* (Col 2:12)

From what sins does Jesus set us free in Baptism?

In Baptism Jesus sets us free from original sin and all personal sins we may have committed before being baptized, as well as all punishment due for sin. (1263)

> *Blessed be the God and Father of our Lord Jesus Christ! In his great mercy we have been reborn to a living hope through the resurrection of Jesus Christ from the dead. . . .* (1 Pt 1:3)

What other effects does Baptism have?

At Baptism we receive sanctifying grace, the theological or God-given virtues, and the seven gifts of the Holy Spirit. We become new creatures, partakers of the divine nature, coheirs with Christ, members of his Church, and temples of the Holy Spirit. (1265–1266)

You see what love the Father has given us so we might be called children of God—and we are! (1 Jn 3:1)

What is the baptismal seal or character?

In Baptism we also receive a permanent spiritual seal called a character, which sets us apart as belonging to Jesus Christ. This character or seal enables us to take part in Christian worship and to witness to Christ. Other sacraments which confer a lasting seal are Confirmation and Holy Orders. (1121, 1272–1274, 1280)

Do not grieve the Holy Spirit, with whom you were sealed for the day of redemption. (Eph 4:30)

How is Baptism given?

Baptism is given by pouring water on the forehead while saying the necessary words: "I baptize you in the name of the Father, and of the Son, and of the Holy Spirit." It also may be given by immersion, which symbolizes dying to sin and rising to new life with Christ. (1284)

The rite of Baptism brings out the sacrament's meaning through various signs and symbols. But the essential part is saying the words at the same time that the water flows on the forehead. (1234–1246)

All authority in heaven and on earth has been given to me. Go, therefore, and make disciples of all nations, baptizing them in the name of the Father and of the Son and of the Holy Spirit. . . . (Mt 28:18–19)

What makes up the sign of Baptism?

The sign of Baptism is made up of water and words. (1278)

What do the water and words stand for?

The water stands for the removal of sin and the giving of new life called grace. The words show that the person is entering a new and lasting relationship with our Triune God—Father, Son, and Holy Spirit. (1228, 1279)

Who may receive Baptism?

Any unbaptized person may receive Baptism. If the person has reached what is called the "age of reason"—the age at which a person is able to understand—he or she must also want to receive the sacrament and have faith and sorrow for sin, with the intention of avoiding future sin. (1246, 1257)

> *Such a life is good and acceptable in the sight of God our Savior, whose wish is that all may be saved and may come to knowledge of the truth.* (1 Tm 2:3–4)

Who are catechumens?

Catechumens are unbaptized persons who are taking instructions to become Catholics. (1247–1249)

Is Baptism necessary?

Baptism is necessary for salvation for everyone who has heard the Good News. Through Baptism our sins are forgiven, we receive the life of grace, are made children of God, and are incorporated into Christ and his Church. (1257)

> *Each of you must repent and be baptized in the name of Jesus Christ for the forgiveness of your sins, and you will receive the gift of the Holy Spirit, for the promise is to you and your children and to all who are far away—anyone the Lord our God calls.* (Acts 2:38–39)

Since Baptism is necessary for salvation, what will happen to those people who, through no fault of their own, have not received it? Can they be saved?

Those who through no fault of their own have not received the sacrament of Baptism can be saved through what is called baptism of blood or baptism of desire. (1258–1260)

What is baptism of blood?

Baptism of blood is the reception of grace by an unbaptized person because the person gives his or her life for love of Christ or a Christian virtue. (1258, 1281)

What is baptism of desire?

Baptism of desire is the reception of grace because of perfect love of God or perfect contrition for sin and the desire to do God's will. In other words, if the person were able to receive the sacrament, he or she would have been baptized. (1259–1260)

How do non-Christians receive salvation?

Anyone who lives a good, upright life, who seeks the truth, or who does the will of God as he or she knows it, can be saved. These persons would ask for Baptism if they knew about it. (1260)

Why does the Church baptize infants?

The Church baptizes infants so that they may be reborn to the divine life of grace in Christ Jesus and become heirs of heaven. (1250–1252)

> *Give thanks to the Father who made you worthy to share in the portion of the saints in light. He has rescued us from the power of darkness and has brought us into the kingdom of his beloved Son, by whom we are redeemed and our sins are forgiven.* (Col 1:12–14)

Should the Baptism of infants be put off for a long time?

Children should be baptized within the first few weeks after birth. Catholic parents who put it off for a long time, or entirely neglect to baptize their children, deprive them of the priceless sacrament of faith. Believing parents desire that their children grow up in Christ, as members of the Church, free of the impediment of original sin. (1250)

> *I say to you, if you are not born of water and the Spirit you cannot enter the kingdom of God. What is born of the flesh is flesh and what is born of the Spirit is spirit.* (Jn 3:5–6)

Should an infant be baptized without the permission of a parent or guardian?

An infant should not be baptized without the permission of a parent or guardian, except when in danger of death. The parent or guardian must see to the Christian upbringing of a baptized child, for the infant is baptized "in the faith of the Church." (1257, 1282)

What happens to infants who die unbaptized?

The Church entrusts these infants to God's mercy. Since God wills that all be saved, it is reasonable to hope that in his mercy he will provide salvation and eternal beatitude. (1261)

> *Let the children come to me! Do not stop them! For of such as these is the kingdom of God.* (Mk 10:14)

Can we be baptized more than once?

No, we can be baptized only once. Due to the permanent spiritual seal we received at Baptism, there is no need to be baptized again. (1272, 1280)

What is conditional Baptism?

Conditional Baptism is giving Baptism on the condition that it can be received (using such words as: "If you are not baptized, I baptize you . . ." or "If you are alive, I baptize you . . ."). This is permitted because Baptism is necessary for salvation.

Do converts have to be baptized again?

Christian converts to the Catholic faith do not have to be baptized again if their first Baptism was valid, that is, given with the use of water (made to flow on the skin), together with the formula of Baptism, performed with the intention of doing what the Church does.

Who may administer the sacrament of Baptism?

The bishop, priest, or deacon is the usual minister of Baptism, but when a person is in danger of death, anyone may and sometimes should baptize. No one, however, may baptize himself or herself. (1256)

In an emergency, does the person who baptizes have to be a Catholic?

In an emergency the person who baptizes can be anyone— man, woman, or child, Catholic or non-Catholic, atheist, or unbeliever—as long as he or she administers the sacrament properly and does it with the intention "to do what the Church does." (1256, 1284)

How is emergency Baptism given?

Emergency Baptism is given by pouring ordinary water three times on the forehead of the person to be baptized, say- ing while pouring it: "I baptize you in the name of the Father, and of the Son, and of the Holy Spirit." The words must be said at the same time the water is poured. (1284)

Is Baptism that is administered by a layperson as valid as that administered by the priest?

Yes. When properly given, Baptism administered by a layperson is as valid as Baptism given by a priest. (1256)

What is the baptismal robe?

The baptismal robe is the white garment given to the newly baptized as a symbol of grace and innocence. (1243)

For all of you who were baptized into Christ have clothed yourselves with Christ. (Gal 3:27)

What is baptismal water?

Baptismal water is water previously blessed for use in Baptism, but in case of emergency, any water may be used. (1238)

What does the candle represent?

The candle represents Christ who has enlightened the newly baptized. Through Christians Christ is the light of the world. (1243)

You are the light of the world. A city cannot be hidden, if it is set atop a mountain. (Mt 5:14)

What is a baptistry?

A baptistry is the part of the Church (or a separate building) in which Baptism takes place. It contains the baptismal font, the place where one is baptized.

What is chrism?

Chrism is a blessed mixture of oil and some aromatic substance used during the baptismal ceremony, in Confirmation, during the ordination of bishops and priests, and in the consecration of churches, altars, etc. It represents the anointing by the Holy Spirit. (1241)

What are the baptismal promises?

The baptismal promises are a renewal of our baptismal commitment. We promise to renounce the devil, his allurements, or temptations, and to live according to the teachings of Christ and his Church. These promises are renewed each year at the Easter Vigil. (1237, 1254)

> *But thanks be to God, for you who were once slaves to sin have become obedient from the heart to the pattern of teaching which was handed down to you—you have been set free from sin and have become slaves of righteousness.* (Rom 6:17–18)

What is a godparent?

A godparent serves as a representative of the community of faith. At Baptism there must be at least one godparent. (1255)

What is the role of godparents?

Godparents are encouraged to help and support the parents in giving the child an adequate formation in faith. Godparents should themselves be good Catholics. (1255)

Should an adult be baptized without a godparent?

An adult should not be baptized without a godparent, for the godparent helps the person to prepare well for Baptism and afterward aids him or her to persevere in the faith and

Christian life. Godparenting is a very ancient custom in the Catholic Church. (1255)

What does the Church require of a godparent?

The Church requires that a godparent be mature enough to take on the responsibility, that he or she be a member of the Catholic Church and have already received Baptism, Confirmation, and Eucharist.

May a non-Catholic act as a godparent?

If the non-Catholic is a baptized and believing Christian, he or she may act as a Christian witness, if this is requested by the parents. In such situations when there is one non-Catholic godparent, a Catholic godparent should also be present. (The norms for various ecumenical cases should be followed.) (1255)

What does a godparent do at the Baptism?

A godparent testifies to the faith of the one to be baptized, or in the case of an infant, the godparent professes the faith of the Church together with the child's parents. (1253)

What is a Christian name?

A Christian name is the name received at Baptism. Parents are encouraged to give their child a saint's name so that the new Christian will have a patron in heaven to imitate and ask for help. The *Catechism of the Catholic Church* states: "The name is the icon of the person. It demands respect as a sign of the dignity of the one who bears it." (2156–2159)

> *To whoever is victorious I will give . . . a white stone with a new name written on it, which no one will know except the one who receives it.* (Rev 2:17)

What does the word "christening" mean?

"Christening" is another name for Baptism. It means "to make like Christ."

What virtues do we receive at Baptism?

At Baptism we receive the theological virtues (faith, hope, and charity) and the cardinal virtues (prudence, justice, temperance, and fortitude). (1266)

Confirmation

What is Confirmation?

Confirmation is the sacrament in which the Holy Spirit comes to us in a special way to join us more closely to Jesus and his Church and to seal and strengthen us as Christ's witnesses. It is the completion of baptismal grace. (1285, 1316)

> When the Intercessor comes, whom I will send to you from the Father—the Spirit of truth that comes forth from the Father—he will bear witness to me, but you, too, will bear witness. . . . (Jn 15:26) (See also Acts 2:4; 8:14–17.)

Who is the minister of Confirmation?

In the Latin Rite the bishop is the ordinary minister of Confirmation, but priests may confirm in certain circumstances when authorized by the bishop. In the Eastern Church the priest ordinarily administers Confirmation at the same time as Baptism. He uses sacred chrism consecrated by the bishop to bring out this sacrament's connection with the apostolic office. (1299, 1312–1313)

> For the one God sent speaks the words of God, for he gives the Spirit without measure. (Jn 3:34)

What does "confirm" mean?

To confirm means to strengthen. In Confirmation our faith is deepened and strengthened, and through this sacrament we are more perfectly bound to Christ and to his Church. (1285)

In Christ you who heard the word of truth—the good news of your salvation—and believed it were sealed by the promised Holy Spirit, which is the pledge that we shall gain our inheritance when God redeems what is his, to the praise of his glory! (Eph 1:13–14)

How is Confirmation given?

In the Latin Rite the bishop extends his hands over the person and anoints the forehead in the form of a cross while saying: "Be sealed with the Gift of the Holy Spirit." The person being confirmed answers "Amen," meaning "Let it be so." The Gift is the Holy Spirit, who is the Gift of the Father and the Son to us. (1299–1301)

Then they laid their hands on them, and they received the Holy Spirit. (Acts 8:17)

What makes up the sign of Confirmation?

The sign of Confirmation is made up of anointing and words. (1293)

What does the action of confirming tell us about the sacrament?

In the action of confirming, the anointing shows that strength and power are being received from the Holy Spirit. This anointing is a sign of our consecration to Jesus Christ. (1294, 1305)

What do we mean by "anointing"?

"Anointing" means "signing with oil." The blessed oil that is used is called chrism, which stands for spiritual strength. The sweet-smelling aromatic substance that it contains stands for freedom from sin and for spreading goodness. (1293–1294, 1297)

> *We are the aroma Christ offers to God among those being saved and among those who are perishing. For some it is a deadly fragrance which leads to death, for others it is a lifegiving fragrance which leads to life.* (2 Cor 2:15–16)

What do the words signify?

The words signify that we are receiving the Holy Spirit in a special way, and are being sealed or marked as Christ's witnesses. (1300)

> *It is God who establishes us in Christ with you and who has anointed us, who has placed his seal on us and given our hearts the Spirit as a down payment.* (2 Cor 1:21–22)

What are the effects of Confirmation?

Confirmed Catholics have become full-fledged members of the Church. They have received spiritual strength and special graces to help them better witness to Christ. The confirmed have also grown in the graces and gifts first received in Baptism. This is indicated during the Confirmation ceremony when the Holy Spirit is called upon to come with his seven gifts. (1303)

> *They prayed over them that they might receive the Holy Spirit, for it had not yet come upon any of them—they had only been baptized in the name of the Lord Jesus.* (Acts 8:15–16)

What are the duties of confirmed Catholics?

Confirmed Catholics are to keep on learning about their faith. They are to live it, love it, stand up for it, and share it as Christ's witnesses. (1303)

What do we mean when we say that a Christian is sealed as Christ's witness?

In Confirmation a Christian receives a second spiritual seal which lasts forever. The first lasting spiritual seal was received at Baptism; Confirmation seals our public commitment to Christ begun in Baptism. This seal is called a character. (1304–1305, 1317)

I am sending the promise of my Father upon you, so stay in the city until you are clothed with power from on high. (Lk 24:49)

Is Confirmation necessary for salvation?

Confirmation is not absolutely necessary for salvation, but it could be seriously wrong to neglect this sacrament because it deepens baptismal grace and brings an abundant outpouring of the Holy Spirit. Baptism, Confirmation, and Eucharist so complement one another that all three are required for full Christian initiation. Confirmation is also important for the growth of the Church. (1306)

Who may receive Confirmation?

Any baptized Catholic who has not been confirmed may receive Confirmation. The Church urges Catholics to study their faith well before receiving Confirmation, because a confirmed Catholic is expected to live up to his or her faith. (1306)

Is there a preferred age for confirming?

In the Latin tradition the person to be confirmed should have reached the age of discretion. Since Confirmation is a free gift, however, one need not be any specific age in order to receive it. In the Eastern Church Confirmation is given to infants immediately after Baptism. (1307–1308)

Can the dying receive Confirmation?

Any priest can give Confirmation to a dying person so that he or she will have received the fullness of Christ. (1307, 1314)

How should a Catholic prepare for Confirmation?

A Catholic should prepare for Confirmation by studying the Catholic faith, by praying, and by witnessing to Christ. The candidate must be in the state of grace and have the same intentions as the Church. (1309–1310)

They all devoted themselves single-mindedly to prayer. . . . (Acts 1:14)

What is the purpose of a Confirmation sponsor?

A Confirmation sponsor has the same duties as a baptismal godparent. The Church suggests that the baptismal godparent become the Confirmation sponsor; however, another sponsor may be chosen. A sponsor must be a Catholic in good standing, already confirmed. (1311)

Is another saint's name taken in Confirmation?

A Catholic may take another saint's name in Confirmation if he or she wishes, in order to invoke the help of that patron saint.

Eucharist

How is Jesus still with us?

Jesus is still with us in his Church, in his Word, in the seven sacraments, in the Christian community, in the needy, and in other ways, but most especially in the Holy Eucharist. (1373)

What is the Holy Eucharist?

The Holy Eucharist is a sacrament, a sacrifice, and the abiding presence of Jesus himself, God and man. Jesus is truly and completely present under the appearances of bread and wine, to make us more like himself and to join us to one another.

I am the bread of life. (Jn 6:35)

Why did Jesus give us the Holy Eucharist?

Jesus gave us the Holy Eucharist because he wanted to stay close to his followers until the end of time to teach us, comfort us, strengthen us, and make us holy. (1323)

Whoever comes to me will not hunger, and whoever believes in me will never thirst. (Jn 6:35)

How is the Eucharist different from all the other sacraments?

The Eucharist is different from all the other sacraments because under the appearances of bread and wine Jesus Christ is completely present as both God and man. It is his Body and Blood. In the other sacraments he is present only by his power and its effects.

I am the living bread that came down from heaven. Anyone who eats of this bread he will live forever, but the bread that I will give for the life of the world is my flesh. (Jn 6:51)

Is the Eucharist important?

Yes, the Eucharist is of the greatest importance. It is "the sum and summary of our faith." (1327–1328)

What do the words of consecration tell us?

The words of consecration said at Mass tell us that the Eucharist is the Body and Blood of Christ and that Christ is offered in sacrifice: "Take this, all of you, and eat of it, for this is my body, which will be given up for you . . . this is the chalice of my blood . . . which will be poured out for you and for many for the forgiveness of sins." (1333)

> *The blessing cup we bless, is it not a sharing in Christ's blood? The bread we break, is it not a sharing in Christ's body?* (1 Cor 10:16)

What is transubstantiation?

Transubstantiation is the changing of the entire substance of bread and wine into Christ's Body and Blood. This takes place at Mass at the moment of the consecration. (1373–1377, 1413)

Why does the Eucharist still look and taste like bread and wine?

Even though the words of consecration change the entire substance of the bread and wine into the Body and Blood of the Lord, the Eucharist still looks and tastes like bread and wine in order to elicit our faith. The change is in the substance (what it actually is); however, the accidents (what it looks and tastes like) remain the same. We say rightly that it is Jesus under the appearance of bread and wine. Jesus wanted to veil his Real Presence and come to us in a way that would be familiar to us, as food. (1333–1336, 1374, 1392, 1404)

> *If anyone eats the bread or drinks from the cup of the Lord unworthily, he will be answerable for the Body and Blood of the Lord.* (1 Cor 11:27)

How can we be sure this transubstantiation really happens?

There is no way that we can prove that transubstantiation really happens at Mass. We know it is true because Jesus said it is so. Our faith is in him. As Son of God he would not empha-size something in his teaching that was not true. As God who created the whole universe from nothing, he can certainly change the nature of something he created. (1375)

If Jesus is present under the species of bread and wine, why do we usually receive only the Host?

Although Jesus is present under both species, the sacra-ment is often given only under the form of bread (the Host) for reasons of practicality, such as fear of spilling the Precious Blood, or for people's uneasiness at sharing a cup with many other people. It is important to remember that the Lord is present under both species. We are not deprived of his Presence by receiving him only under one form. It is more perfect, how-ever, to receive the Eucharist under both species because it is more clearly and completely a sign of communion. (1390)

What is *Corpus Christi?*

Corpus Christi is Latin for the "Body of Christ." It is also a feast day the Church dedicates to giving praise and thanks to the Holy Eucharist in a special way; it is celebrated on the second Sunday after Pentecost (in the United States and Canada).

What is the Mass or Eucharistic Celebration?

The Mass or Eucharistic Celebration is:
- ❖ the sacrifice of the cross taking place today on our altars;
- ❖ a memorial of the death, resurrection, and ascension of Jesus;
- ❖ a sacred banquet in which the food we receive is Jesus himself. (1329–1330)

What does the word "Eucharist" mean?

The word Eucharist, which we use for Christ fully present under the appearances of bread and wine, means "thanksgiving." (1328)

> *The Lord Jesus on the night when he was betrayed took bread, and when he had given thanks, he broke it, and said, "This is my body which is for you. . . ."* (1 Cor 11:23–24 RSV)

Why do we call the Eucharistic Celebration the "Mass"?

The word "Mass" comes from the Latin word *missa* which means "sending" (*missio*). At the end of every Mass we are sent forth, commissioned to announce the Good News with our own lives. (1332)

What are some other names for the Mass?

Other names for the Mass include the Lord's Supper, the Eucharistic assembly, the memorial of the Lord's Passion and resurrection, the holy Sacrifice, the Liturgy, the Eucharistic Celebration, Eucharistic Sacrifice, and Breaking of Bread. Liturgy means "service." (1328–1332)

How can Jesus be truly present at so many Masses at once?

Jesus is truly present at every Mass all over the world because each priest has the power to consecrate the Eucharist. Christ's Body and Blood are present in a way that is not subject to conditions of space and time. Jesus wants to make himself available to all of us, as he prophesied:

> *And when I am lifted up from the earth I will draw all men to myself.* (Jn 12:32)

When was the Eucharist first celebrated?

Jesus celebrated the first Eucharist at the Last Supper on Holy Thursday evening, the night before he died. (1339)

Then he took bread, blessed it, broke it, and gave it to them, saying, "This is my body which is given up for you—do this in my remembrance." Likewise he took the cup after they had eaten and said, "This cup is the new covenant in my blood which is poured out for you." (Lk 22:19–20)

Who were present at the first Eucharistic Celebration?

The apostles were present at the first Eucharistic Celebration. (1340)

When the hour came he sat down at table with the apostles. (Lk 22:14)

How does Christ renew the sacrifice of the cross?

For our sake Christ renews the sacrifice of the cross in an unbloody manner at Mass. (1337, 1367)

He is always alive to intercede for them. (Heb 7:25)

Why does Christ renew his sacrifice today?

Christ renews his sacrifice for us and for our world today so that he can remain with us throughout history, and so that through him, with him, and in him, we can adore and thank the Father and ask his forgiveness and help. (1341–1344, 1356–1358)

He presented himself as an unblemished offering to God and will purify our consciences from ineffective practices so that we will be fit to worship the living God. (Heb 9:14)

Why is Jesus called the Lamb of God at every Eucharistic Celebration?

Jesus is called the Lamb of God because he was slain like the Passover Lamb, and his Paschal Mystery saved us from the slavery of sin. (608)

Christ our Paschal Lamb has been sacrificed. (1 Cor 5:7) (See also Is 53:7; Jn 1:36; Rev 5:12.)

What are the main purposes of the Mass?

Through the Mass, the Church offers praise, adoration, and thanksgiving to God the Father. As the memorial of Christ's sacrifice, the Mass is offered in reparation for sins, and in it we ask God's help for ourselves and others. (1358, 1407, 1414)

What roles do the priest and people have at Mass?

All the people gathered together in the Eucharistic assembly participate in the Mass. Some fulfill specific roles such as reader, gift bearer, or Eucharistic minister, while the whole community offers the assent of mind and heart. The priest presides over the celebration. He alone acts in the person of Christ the Head, who is always the invisible high priest. (1348)

> *Therefore, since we have a great high priest who has passed through the heavens—Jesus the Son of God—let us hold fast to the faith we profess.* (Heb 4:14)

What are the presidential prayers of the Mass?

They are the prayers that can be said only by a priest as presider, for example, the Eucharistic Prayer.

What are the fruits of participating in the Mass with attention and love?

The Eucharist builds up the Church in unity and love, drawing us closer together in Christ. It helps us grow in the love of God and neighbor, especially the poor. Through it we grow spiritually, are strengthened to avoid sin, and obtain graces and blessings. We also receive a pledge of the glory to come in eternal life. (1391–1405)

Why is the Mass so important?

In the Mass Jesus himself is made present and prays to the Father for us. He renews his redemptive sacrifice, which is the only worship truly worthy of God's honor and glory. (1324)

Are Catholics obliged to participate in the Mass?

Because of the importance of the Mass, the Church obliges us to participate in the Mass on Sundays and holy days of obligation. (See pages 237–238 for a listing of the holy days in the United States.) (1389)

Should a Catholic ever stop going to Mass?

No Catholic should stop going to Mass, for any reason. Even persons who cannot receive Holy Communion (for example, because of remarriage after a divorce) should participate in the Mass to fulfill their duty to worship God and to ask his help and mercy.

The Celebration of the Eucharist

What are the introductory rites of the Mass?

The introductory rites of the Mass include the Entrance Chant, the Greeting, the Rite for the Blessing and Sprinkling of Water, the Penitential Act, the Kyrie, the Gloria, and the Collect (the opening prayer). The introductory rites prepare the faith community to hear God's Word and to participate at the Eucharist.

What is the Entrance Chant?

The Entrance Chant is a short prayer that is sung or recited as the priest and servers enter.

What is the Greeting?

While all are standing the priest leads the assembly in the Sign of the Cross and greets them in God's name. Those assembled reply with the words: "And with your spirit."

What is the Rite for the Blessing and Sprinkling of Water at Mass?

The Rite for the Blessing and Sprinkling of Water may be used at Mass instead of the Penitential Act. By being sprinkled with holy water, we are reminded of our Baptism.

What is the Penitential Act of the Mass?

In the Penitential Act of the Mass, we call to mind our sins and ask God to have mercy on us, so that we may be better disposed to celebrate the Eucharist. (1393–1395)

What is the Kyrie?

Kyrie eleison is Greek for "Lord, have mercy." This call to God for mercy is alternated with *Christe eleison* ("Christ, have mercy") following the Penitential Act.

What is the Gloria?

The *Gloria in excelsis* ("Glory to God in the highest") is an ancient hymn of praise sung or recited by all on Sundays and other solemnities and feasts outside of Advent and Lent.

What is the Collect?

The Collect is the opening prayer recited by the priest, expressing the theme of the particular celebration. The people respond with "Amen."

What is the Liturgy of the Word?

The Liturgy of the Word is a main part of the Mass that includes readings from Scripture, the Responsorial Psalm, the Alleluia or Gospel Acclamation, the Homily, the Profession of Faith, and the Universal Prayer. (1346, 1349)

What Scripture readings are used at Mass?

On Sundays, the first reading is taken from the Old Testament, and the second is from the New Testament; the Gospel follows. On weekdays, there is one reading taken from either the Old or New Testament, followed by the Gospel.

What is the Responsorial Psalm?

The Responsorial Psalm is a psalm or sacred song prayed by the worshipping community as a response to the first reading during the Liturgy of the Word.

What is the Homily?

In the Homily the priest or deacon explains the Word of God just proclaimed. (1349)

When you received the word of God that you heard from us you did not accept it as mere human words but for what it truly is, the word of God which is at work in you believers. (1 Thes 2:13)

What is the Profession of Faith proclaimed at the Mass?

On Sundays and holy days, the Profession of Faith or Creed is said by the faithful to express belief in the truths of our Catholic faith and in the Word of God proclaimed in the readings.

What is the Universal Prayer?

The Universal Prayer, also known as the prayer of the faithful or general intercessions, is a special prayer by which the faithful act as a priestly people and intercede, or ask God's help, for the needs of the Church and the world. (1349)

> *I urge that supplications, prayers, intercessions, and thanksgivings be made for all men—for kings and for all those in positions of authority—that we may lead a peaceful, quiet life, holy and respectable in every way.* (1 Tm 2:1–2)

What is the Liturgy of the Eucharist?

The Liturgy of the Eucharist follows the Liturgy of the Word, and together they form one great act of worship. Within the Eucharistic Prayer, our gifts of bread and wine become the Body and Blood of Christ, offered in sacrifice to God. At Communion, we receive Jesus as a sign of our unity with Christ and with one another. (1346)

What is the Presentation and Preparation of the Gifts?

During this rite the altar is prepared, the gifts of bread and wine are carried to it and then offered to God, and the priest washes his hands and prays to be cleansed of sin. The offering of the gifts may be accompanied by the Offertory Chant, an appropriate song sung by the choir or the assembled faithful. (1350)

> *Therefore, let us continually offer through him a sacrifice of praise to God, the fruit of lips that acknowledge his name.* (Heb 13:15)

What is the Preface of the Mass?

The Preface of the Mass is a prayer of praise and thanks to God our Father for the work of salvation or for some particular aspect of his saving love. At every Mass the prayer ends with the Preface Acclamation, also called the Sanctus, that is, the acclamation "Holy, Holy, Holy," a wonderful song in which priest and people join their praise of God to that of the angels. (1352)

What is the Eucharistic Prayer?

The Eucharistic Prayer is an extended hymn of thanksgiving to God for his work of salvation. Within this great prayer, bread and wine are changed into the Body and Blood of Christ. (1352–1353)

What is the Institution narrative and Consecration of the Mass?

The Institution narrative is that part of the Eucharistic Prayer in which the priest recalls the words and actions of Jesus when he gathered the disciples at table. The heart of the Eucharistic Prayer is the Consecration, when at the words of the priest—"This is my Body"; "This is the chalice of my Blood"—bread and wine become the Body and Blood of Christ. All those present adore the Real Presence of the Lord. (1353)

What is the Mystery of Faith, or Memorial Acclamation?

After the Consecration the priest announces "The Mystery of Faith," inviting us to acknowledge what we have witnessed. We respond with these words: "We proclaim your Death, O Lord, and profess your Resurrection until you come again," or a similar acclamation. (1354)

Are Masses offered for particular people?

Yes, Masses are usually offered for the intentions of a specific person either living or deceased. Also during the Eucharistic Prayer, a series of intercessions are prayed for the Holy Father, the bishop, priests, deacons, and all the faithful throughout the world. These intercessions unite us with the universal Church. (1354)

What is the Concluding Doxology?

The Concluding Doxology is a tribute of praise to our Triune God proclaimed through, with, and in Christ. It concludes the Eucharistic Prayer; the Communion Rite follows.

What is the Communion Rite?

The Communion Rite includes the Lord's Prayer, the Sign of Peace, the Fraction or breaking of the Bread (the Lamb of God), the Communion of the priest and people, and the Prayer after Communion. (1355)

What is the Sign of Peace?

The Sign of Peace is the expression of the love and peace which members of the community give each other at Mass before sharing the Body and Blood of Christ.

What is the Fraction of the Bread?

The Fraction of the Bread is when the priest breaks the Host as a sign that in Communion we become one in the Body and Blood of Christ. At this moment we pray aloud the Lamb of God to express our gratitude and unworthiness.

What is Holy Communion?

Holy Communion is the real Eucharistic Jesus whom we receive at Mass. (1382, 1384)

Unless you eat the flesh of the Son of Man and drink his blood, you do not have life within you. (Jn 6:53)

What are the Concluding Rites of the Mass?

The Concluding Rites of the Mass include a Solemn Blessing or Prayer over the People, the Final Blessing by the priest, and the Dismissal of the people, inviting them to do good works and to praise God.

What is the Extraordinary Form of the Mass?

This refers to the celebration of the Mass in Latin according to the Roman Missal of 1962, that is, before the reforms of the Second Vatican Council. On July 7, 2007, Pope Benedict XVI gave permission for a wider use of this form for those who may wish it.

Receiving the Eucharist

Why does Jesus come to us in the Eucharist?

Jesus comes to us in the Eucharist to give us new spiritual energy so that we can continue leading good Christian lives. (1391–1392)

Just as the living Father sent me, and I live because of the Father, so too, whoever feeds on me will live because of me. (Jn 6:57)

Do we need the help of the Eucharist?

The Eucharist fortifies and sustains us. Temptations and difficulties can "wear us down" in spirit. Communion helps us to go ahead with new strength and courage. Receiving the Eucharist, we are more united to Christ and we also grow in love for all God's people. The Eucharist joins the whole Church more closely together, for through it each member grows in grace and overcomes sin. (1393–1398)

How should we prepare ourselves to receive the Holy Eucharist?

We must believe that Jesus is really present in the Holy Eucharist, be free from serious sin, and observe the fast before receiving Holy Communion. In addition, we should desire this union with Christ and try to grow in our love for God and others. (1385–1387)

Lord, I am not worthy to have you come under my roof—just say the word and my servant will be healed. (Mt 8:8)

How long must one fast before receiving Holy Communion?

The Church requires a fast of one hour from all solid foods and liquids, both alcoholic and non-alcoholic (with the exception of water, which can be taken at any time, and medicine).

Are there any exceptions to the Eucharistic fast?

The elderly and the ill, as well as those who care for them, need only fast for fifteen minutes before receiving Communion.

How should a person receive the Eucharist?

A person should receive the Eucharist with faith, reverence, and love. We show our faith by answering "Amen" after the priest, deacon, or lay minister has said, "The Body of Christ." We show our reverence by the respectful way we receive Communion. We show our love by our prayerful union with Jesus and by carrying his love into our daily actions. (1378, 1387)

What are the rights and privileges of Catholics who have made their first Communion?

Catholics who have made their first Communion have become active members of the worshipping community. They may receive Communion often—even daily—provided they are properly disposed. (1388)

What are the duties and responsibilities of Catholics who have made their first Communion?

Catholics who have made their first Communion are to take part in the Mass every Sunday (or Saturday evening) and receive Communion at least once a year (usually between the first Sunday in Lent and Trinity Sunday). This is known as the Easter duty. For a good reason the precept may be fulfilled at another time during the year. (1389)

May a non-Catholic receive Communion?

Because the Eucharist is the premier sign of our unity in Christ, receiving Communion testifies to unity of faith and worship. The Catholic Church cannot invite non-Catholics to receive Communion, since they do not share the same faith. In certain circumstances, however, the bishop may permit some other Christians to receive Communion if they truly believe what Catholics do about the sacrament and sincerely ask for it. (1398–1401)

What is Viaticum?

Viaticum is Communion given to a person in danger of death. It should be given when the sick are fully conscious. (1517)

Jesus Remains in the Tabernacle

Does the Eucharist remain in the church after Mass?

The Eucharist does remain in the church after Mass, in the box-like shrine called a tabernacle. (1379)

How should we show our love and thankfulness to Jesus for remaining in the tabernacle?

We can do this by making frequent visits to church, by being respectful and prayerful, by participating often in the Eucharistic Celebration, and attending parish devotions. (1374)

What is a sanctuary lamp?

A sanctuary lamp is a candle that continuously burns near the tabernacle where the Blessed Sacrament is kept, indicating the presence of the Lord.

Is prayer before the Blessed Sacrament beneficial?

Prayer before the Blessed Sacrament brings great comfort and strength, because in the Eucharist Jesus is fully present. He is there to listen to us and help us. (1380–1381, 1418)

Jesus, knowing that his hour had come to leave this world for the Father, having loved his own in the world, he loved them to the end. (Jn 13:1)

What is Eucharistic Benediction?

Eucharistic Benediction is the ceremony in which the priest blesses the people with the consecrated Host enclosed in a sacred vessel called a monstrance. The monstrance has a round window that makes the Host visible to the worshipping community.

How do we reverence the Blessed Sacrament?

We show reverence to the Blessed Sacrament either by a genuflection (bending the right knee to the floor) or by a deep bow. These signs of reverence are shown when entering one's place in church and when passing in front of the Blessed Sacrament.

Liturgical Vessels and Vestments Used at Mass

What are vestments?

Vestments are special robes worn to celebrate the Eucharist and the other sacraments. Usually the priest celebrating Mass wears the chasuble, alb, and stole.

What is a chasuble?

A chasuble is the outer vestment of the priest celebrating Mass. It comes in different colors and often is decorated with religious symbols.

What is an alb?

An alb is a long white tunic or robe that the priest wears under the chasuble while offering the Eucharistic Sacrifice.

What is a stole?

A stole is a long, narrow band of the same material and color as the chasuble. The priest wears the stole around his neck and hanging down in front. The deacon wears a stole over his left shoulder and drawn across the chest to the right side, where it is fastened.

What is a cincture?

The cincture is a long cord used to gather the alb at the priest's waist.

What is a dalmatic?

The dalmatic, a vestment similar to a chasuble, is worn by the deacon over the alb and stole at liturgical celebrations.

What is an altar?

An altar is the table of the Lord, made of marble, granite, wood, or another solid, attractive material. It occupies the central position in the church sanctuary.
The People of God are called together to share in the offering of the Lord Jesus at this altar of sacrifice. Usually, relics of martyrs or saints are put inside the altar. (1383)

Why is the crucifix placed on the altar or near it?

The crucifix reminds the worshipping community of the sacrifice of Jesus on the cross.

What meaning do the lighted candles have?

The lighted candles witness to our devotion to Jesus who is light and life with his grace.

What is a lectern?

A lectern is a stand from which the Liturgy of the Word is proclaimed.

What is a lector?

A lector is the person who proclaims God's Word (other than the Gospel) at Mass.

What kind of bread must be used to celebrate the Eucharist?

The bread used to celebrate the Eucharist must be made only of wheat flour and water. Nothing else may be substituted or added. (1412)

What kind of wine must be used to celebrate the Eucharist?

Pure, natural grape wine must be used to celebrate the Eucharist. Such wine, made for sacramental purposes, should be clearly designated as altar wine. (1412)

What are the cruets?

The cruets are small pitchers containing the wine and water used during the Eucharistic Celebration.

What is the chalice?

The chalice is the sacred cup in which the wine becomes the true Blood of Christ at the consecration.

What is a ciborium?

A ciborium is a cup with a matching lid, used to hold the Body of Christ that will be given in Holy Communion.

What is a corporal?

A corporal is a piece of linen cloth on which rest the vessels holding the Body and Blood of Christ during Mass.

What is a pall?

A pall is a linen card about six inches square, used to cover the chalice containing the precious Blood.

What is a paten?

A paten is the dish upon which the bread, and, later, the consecrated Host is placed.

What is a purificator?

A purificator is a small linen towel that the priest uses to cleanse the sacred vessels.

What is a finger towel?

A finger towel is another small piece of linen that the priest uses to dry his fingers after the rite of washing following the preparation of the gifts.

What books are used at Mass?

The Roman Missal is the book containing the priest's part of the Mass except for the scriptural readings and psalm responsories, which are printed in a book called the lectionary. A large book of the Gospels may also be used.

In regard to the Mass, what do we mean by the word "option"?

Options are choices the Church permits the priest to select from at Mass. For example, he may use one of several Eucharistic Prayers.

Sacraments of Healing

Penance and Reconciliation

What is the sacrament of Penance and Reconciliation?

Penance and Reconciliation is the sacrament of God's loving forgiveness by which we are set free from sin and reconciled with God and the Church, which we have wounded by our sins. This sacrament helps us to grow in God's grace, and it strengthens us to avoid sin and to lead holier lives. (1422)

Be merciful, as your Father is merciful. (Lk 6:36)

From whom do we receive the gift of this sacrament?

We receive the gift of the sacrament of Penance and Reconciliation from Jesus, who gave the apostles the power to forgive sins. (1441)

He breathed on them, and said to them, "Receive the Holy Spirit. If you forgive the sins of any, they are forgiven; if you retain the sins of any, they are retained." (Jn 20:22–23 RSV)

Who may receive the sacrament of Penance and Reconciliation?

Any Catholic who has committed sin may receive the sacrament of Penance and Reconciliation. (1446)

How do we know that God is willing to forgive sins?

We know that God is willing to forgive sins because in the Gospel Jesus has told us this many times and in many ways. (1489)

For the Son of Man came to seek out and save what was lost. (Lk 19:10)

Can every sin be forgiven?

Yes, every sin can be forgiven through the sacrament of Penance. Jesus said to the apostles:

I will give you the keys to the kingdom of heaven, and whatever you bind on earth will have been bound in heaven, and whatever you loose on earth will have been loosed in heaven. (Mt 16:19)

How is the sacrament of Penance given?

The sacrament of Penance is given when we go to confession with sorrow for sin, accept the penance that the priest gives, and receive absolution: "I absolve you from your sins in the name of the Father, and of the Son, and of the Holy Spirit." As when receiving the Eucharist and Confirmation, we answer, "Amen." (1448–1449)

What makes up the sign of the sacrament of Penance?

The sign of Penance is made up of three "acts of the penitent," plus the words of the priest.

Who is a penitent?

A penitent is someone who is sorry for his or her sins.

Father, I have sinned against heaven and before you. (Lk 15:18)

What are the three acts of the penitent?

The penitent's three acts are contrition (sorrow), confession (telling our sins), and satisfaction (making up for the harm done when possible, and doing or saying the penance given by the priest). We also may perform or say other penances beyond what is required. (1450)

What steps does a person follow in receiving this sacrament?

To receive this sacrament with spiritual profit, a person must first examine his or her conscience, then be sincerely sorry for sin, resolving to avoid it in the future. This sorrow is based on spiritual motives such as love of God and hatred of sin. The person then confesses the sins and accepts the penance. (1450, 1460)

What is perfect contrition?

Perfect contrition is sorrow for sin especially because sin displeases God, who is all-good and loving, and deserves all our love. (1452)

What is imperfect contrition?

Imperfect contrition is sorrow for sin for reasons that are good but not the very best, such as sorrow based more on fear than on love. (1453)

What does one do after receiving this sacrament?

One who has received the sacrament of Penance and Reconciliation must say or do the penance given by the priest, avoid everything that would lead to sin, and make up as much as possible and necessary for the harm done. How the harm is to be made up for is explained under various commandments, such as the seventh and eighth. (1459)

Who acts for Jesus in this sacrament?

The priest acts for Jesus in the sacrament of Penance and Reconciliation. When we confess our sins to the priest, we are confessing them to Jesus, who forgives us through the priest. (1461)

> *All this is from God, who reconciled us to himself through Christ and has given us this ministry of reconciliation.* (2 Cor 5:18)

What is the seal of confession?

The seal of confession is the most solemn obligation of a priest to keep secret what has been revealed to him in confession. The priest may never break this seal even to save his own life. (1467)

Should we ever speak of what we heard or said in confession?

With regard to overhearing someone else's confession, we are strictly bound to secrecy; regarding our own confession, we are not. It is better, however, not to talk about the advice given, the penance, etc.

Should we ever be so embarrassed that we do not go to confession?

Embarrassment or fear should not keep us from this sacrament, for the Lord awaits us with love despite our sins. The priest is Christ's representative, bound by the seal of confession never to reveal anything told to him in the confessional. Also, we are free to confess to any priest. (1465)

What does absolution mean?

Absolution means "releasing." Through this sacrament, we are released from our sins—set free from them. (1449)

He who conceals his transgressions will not prosper, but he who confesses and forsakes them will obtain mercy. (Prov 28:13)

Does the priest ever refuse absolution?

A priest could refuse absolution only in rare cases, for example, if the person is not sorry for his or her serious sins, or has no intention of avoiding them in the future, or has no confidence in God's forgiving Spirit. This is what Jesus referred to when he spoke of sin which cannot be forgiven. Unless there is true sorrow, there is no forgiveness. We must have confidence in God's mercy and pray to his Spirit for a contrite heart.

Every sin and blasphemy will be forgiven you, but blasphemy against the Spirit will not be forgiven. (Mt 12:31)

Are there any sins which the ordinary confessor cannot absolve?

Some sins are so grave that the sinner is excommunicated. Absolution in these cases must be sought from the Pope, the bishop, or a priest authorized by them. The exception to this occurs in the danger of death when any priest, even one deprived of permission to hear confessions, can give absolution for all sin and excommunication. (1463)

What is a penance?

A penance is something that must be done or accepted to make up for confessed sin. It should correspond to the type of sins and their gravity. Penances generally take the form of prayer, acts of mercy, or self-denial. (1459–1460)

Return to me with all your heart, with fasting, with weeping, and with mourning; and rend your hearts and not your garments. (Joel 2:12)

Who is a confessor?

The word "confessor" has two meanings: It can mean a priest who hears confessions, or in another unrelated sense, it can mean a saint, other than a martyr, who witnessed to ("confessed") the faith. (1466)

When must a person receive the sacrament of Penance?

A Catholic who has committed a mortal or serious sin must receive the sacrament of Penance. A mortal sin can be forgiven even before confession if a person has perfect (pure) sorrow for having offended our loving God. But normally, he or she must still go to confession before receiving Holy Communion. If we have committed serious sin, we should go to confession soon. (1456)

What should a person do who has committed a mortal sin?

A person who has committed a mortal sin should say a prayer of perfect sorrow with the intention of going to confession soon. This obtains forgiveness and God's grace. But the person must go to confession before receiving Communion.

Are there any requirements for confessing mortal sins?

In confessing mortal sins, a person should say what kind of sins they were and—as far as possible—tell how many times these sins were committed, as well as any circumstances that might alter their nature.

Can a person confess sins with the intention of committing them again?

A person cannot confess sins with the intention of committing them again. No sin is forgiven by God unless there is true sorrow for it (even imperfect sorrow, such as fear of divine punishment) and a firm resolution not to commit it again.

How often must we receive the sacrament of Penance and Reconciliation?

The Church requires us to receive the sacrament of Penance and Reconciliation at least once a year if we have serious sins. It is a good idea to receive this sacrament more frequently because it greatly helps our spiritual growth. (1456–1457)

Why is it beneficial to receive this sacrament frequently, even if we have committed only venial sins?

This sacrament helps us to realize that every sin offends God. It helps us develop greater self-knowledge, grow in grace and love of God and neighbor, and grow spiritually as a living and active member of the Church. (1458)

When may general absolution be given?

In certain rare cases, such as during a war or a natural disaster, general absolution may be given to a group without individual confession. As always, the penitents must be sorry and intend not to sin again. One whose grave sins are forgiven by a general absolution is obliged to make an individual confession as soon as possible before receiving another general absolution, unless a just reason intervenes. (1483)

What is a communal celebration of the sacrament of Penance and Reconciliation?

A communal celebration of this sacrament consists of a common preparation including Scripture readings, a homily, an examination of conscience, individual confession and absolution, and a common request for forgiveness and thanksgiving. This form expresses clearly the ecclesial nature of the sacrament. (1483)

What are the effects of this sacrament?

This sacrament reconciles us with God, who forgives all our sins. We are restored to God's grace and friendship (if this had been broken through serious sin), or our union with him is deepened. We are also reconciled with the Church, which we have wounded by our sins. The sacrament gives us the grace we need to live our Christian life more deeply, thus preparing ourselves for a merciful judgment when we die. (1468–1470)

> *This brother of yours was dead, and has come back to life; he was lost, and has been found!* (Lk 15:32)

How is an examination of conscience made?

An examination of conscience is made by recalling how one has lived up to one's commitment to Christ in thoughts, words, and actions, as well as how one's duties were accomplished. As a help, the Ten Commandments can be recalled one by one, as well as the special duties of Catholic Christians and one's own particular duties. (1454)

In addition, some questions like the following will help us:

- ❖ What is my attitude toward the sacrament of God's mercy, the sacrament of Penance and Reconciliation?

- ❖ Do I want my sins forgiven, so that I can begin a new life and deepen my friendship with God?

- ❖ Did I deliberately conceal serious sins in past confessions through fear or shame? If so, now I want to tell them sincerely, trusting that God will forgive me as he forgave the prodigal son.

- ❖ Did I perform the penance I was given during my last confession? Did I make up for any injuries I caused others?

- ❖ Have I really been trying to become a better Catholic, the way the Gospel teaches?

How Much Do I Love God?

❖ Do I love God and show it by obeying the Ten Commandments?

❖ Do I think about pleasing God, and try to live every day as well as I can?

❖ Do I believe in God and trust him?

❖ Do I accept what the Catholic Church teaches?

❖ Do I try to grow in knowledge and love of my Catholic faith?

❖ Am I courageous in professing my faith in God and the Church?

❖ Am I happy to be a Catholic, willing to be known as one?

❖ Do I turn to God often during the day, especially when I am tempted?

❖ Do I love and reverence God's name? Did I ever take his name in vain?

❖ Did I blaspheme or swear falsely?

❖ Did I show disrespect for our Lady and the saints?

❖ Do I participate at Mass with attention and devotion on Sundays and holy days?

❖ Have I fulfilled the precept of Communion during the Easter season?

❖ Are there "false gods" in my life—money, clothes, superstition, desire for popularity, for example—that actually mean more to me than God does?

How Much Do I Love My Neighbor?

❖ Do I really love my neighbor, or do I use people for my own ends? Do I do to them what I would not want done to myself?

❖ Have I given bad example by my words or actions? Do I contribute to the happiness of every member of my family?

❖ Am I loving and respectful to my parents, my spouse, my children?

❖ If I am permitted, am I willing to share my possessions with those who have less, or do I look down on them?

❖ Do I share in the apostolic and charitable works of my parish?

❖ Do I pray for the needs of the Church and the world?

❖ Am I hardworking and conscientious in fulfilling my duties?

❖ Am I truthful and fair? Did I ever damage another's good name?

❖ Have I ever damaged another person's property or possessions? Have I stolen?

❖ Have I quarreled? Insulted others?

❖ Do I harbor hatred and a thirst for revenge?

How Is My Personal Growth in the Christian Life?

❖ Do I think about heaven and hope for eternal life with God?

❖ Do I pray often? Do I read God's Word, the Bible, and reflect on it?

❖ Do I receive the sacraments of Penance and Holy Eucharist regularly?

❖ Am I pure in my thoughts, words, desires, actions?

❖ Do I keep away from indecent literature, movies, or other forms of entertainment that do not respect God's gift of sexuality?

❖ Do I know how to give of myself for others? Do I try
   to grow spiritually? Can I look at myself honestly to see
   where I can grow?

❖ Am I lazy? Do I waste a lot of time?

❖ Do I use my talents and time to help others know
   Jesus?

Indulgences

What is an indulgence?

An indulgence is the removal of some or all of the temporal punishment due for sins already forgiven. (1471)

What is temporal punishment?

Every sin is a disordered act that has an effect on the sinner. It turns our hearts away from God and toward some
created good instead. The sinner needs purification from these
disordered inclinations. More than a punishment, this purification is a natural consequence of the evil of sin. (1472)

How many kinds of indulgences are there?

There are two kinds of indulgences, *plenary*, which removes
all the temporal punishment due, and *partial*, which shortens
or lessens that punishment.

How often can a plenary indulgence be acquired?

A plenary indulgence can be acquired only once a day,
unless at the point of death.

What is required to gain a plenary indulgence?

To gain a plenary indulgence we must perform the good
work, prayer, or penance to which the indulgence is attached,

go to confession, receive Communion, pray for the intentions of the Pope, and be detached from all sin. If the above requirements for a plenary indulgence are not fulfilled, the indulgence will be only partial.

When may the conditions for receiving a plenary indulgence be met?

Although it is permitted that the conditions be fulfilled several days before or after the work is performed, it is more appropriate to receive Communion and pray for the intentions of the Pope the same day.

How is the condition of praying for the intentions of the Pope met?

The condition of praying for the intentions of the Pope is met by saying an "Our Father" and a "Hail Mary." However, one may add any other prayers or devotions for his intentions.

Can bishops grant a plenary indulgence to their faithful who live where it is impossible, or at least very difficult for them to receive the sacraments of Penance and Holy Eucharist?

Yes, bishops can grant plenary indulgences to these faithful who cannot confess and receive Communion, as long as they are sorry for their sins and intend to receive these sacraments as soon as possible.

Can an indulgence be acquired with the use of a religious article?

Yes, a partial indulgence can be acquired by anyone who uses with devotion a blessed religious article such as a crucifix, rosary, medal, or scapular. If blessed by the Pope or bishop, a religious article can be used to acquire a plenary indulgence on the feast of the holy Apostles Peter and Paul (June 29), as long as the person acquiring the indulgence makes a profession of faith using an official formula such as the Apostles' Creed, the Nicene Creed, etc.

What is the source of indulgences?

Indulgences are granted from the Church's "treasury" or spiritual goods. Because the Church is Christ's Mystical Body, all the members share the same life. The Church's treasury includes the infinite merits of Christ, the prayers and good works of the Blessed Virgin, the saints, and of all the faithful throughout the ages. (1474–1477)

> God's grace and the free gift through the grace of the one man Jesus Christ have overflowed to far greater effect for the many. (Rom 5:15)

Can we gain indulgences for others besides ourselves?

We cannot gain indulgences for other living persons, but we can gain them for the souls in purgatory. (1479)

In the Bible we read that Judas Maccabeus ". . . made atonement for the dead, that they might be delivered from their sin" (2 Mc 12:45).

Why does the Church grant indulgences?

The Church was entrusted with the power of loosing and binding and so willingly opens the treasury of the Lord's redemption and the merits of the saints to help remit our sins. By requiring us to say prayers and do penance and works of charity in order to gain these indulgences, the Church teaches us to take some responsibility for our own salvation. (1478)

Anointing of the Sick

What is the Anointing of the Sick?

The Anointing of the Sick is the sacrament by which Christ comforts and strengthens those who are dangerously ill due to sickness, injury, or old age. (1499, 1511, 1520)

They drove out many demons and anointed many sick people with oil and cured them. (Mk 6:13)

Who acts for Jesus in the Anointing of the Sick?

The priest acts for Jesus in the Anointing of the Sick. (1516)

Is anyone among you sick? He should call the elders of the church, and have them pray over him and anoint him with oil in the name of the Lord—prayer rooted in faith will save whoever is ill and the Lord will raise him up, and even if he has sinned the Lord will forgive him. (Jas 5:14–15)

What makes up the sign of the Anointing of the Sick?

The sign of the Anointing of the Sick is made up of anointing and words. (1518–1519)

How is the Anointing of the Sick given?

The Anointing of the Sick is given by the priest who anoints the sick person on the forehead and hands, saying the appropriate prayers. (1513)

What is the blessed oil that is used in Anointing?

The blessed oil that is used in Anointing is called the oil of the sick. It stands for healing—chiefly spiritual healing, but also physical healing. (1513)

What do the words of the sacrament of Anointing signify?

The words of the sacrament of Anointing signify that we are asking the Lord to give his strength, healing, and grace. The priest says: "Through this holy anointing may the Lord in his love and mercy help you with the grace of the Holy Spirit. May the Lord who frees you from sin save you and raise you up." (1513)

I am the Lord, your healer. (Ex 15:26)

What does this sacrament do for a person?

Through this sacrament, the Holy Spirit strengthens the sick person to deal with the difficulties of illness. The sacrament forgives sins and sometimes can result in physical healing. The sick person is united with Christ's passion, so that the sufferings borne take on new meaning. This spiritually benefits the whole Church. Finally, for those who are approaching death, Anointing prepares them for this final journey. (1520–1523)

I rejoice in what I am suffering for you now: in my flesh I am completing what is lacking in Christ's afflictions on behalf of his body, that is, the church. (Col 1:24)

Why are not all those who are anointed physically healed?

The sacrament of the Anointing is a sacrament of preparation, of consolation, of compassion, of inner healing. Through this anointing the Lord wants to strengthen the sick, to redeem their sufferings, and to prepare them for the final resurrection. Sometimes this sacrament may lead to physical healing, but if not, the sick are still strengthened in Christ. (1518–1519)

If we have died with him we will also live with him: if we endure we will also reign with him. (2 Tm 2:11–12)

Who may receive the Anointing of the Sick?

Any baptized Catholic who is dangerously ill due to sickness, injury, or old age may receive the Anointing of the Sick, even though there is no apparent danger of death. The sacrament should be received when the sick person is best able to profit from it, and not be delayed until the person is at the point of death. Sick children, too, may receive this sacrament if they are old enough to be comforted by it. It can even be given to someone who is unconscious. The elderly who are in a weakened condition are also encouraged by the Church to receive Anointing, even though no dangerous illness is present. (1514)

Where is the sacrament of the Anointing received?

The sacrament of the Anointing is often received at home or in a hospital. It may also be received during a Mass in which there is a communal celebration of the sacrament. (1517)

What is necessary to receive this sacrament worthily?

To receive this sacrament worthily, one should be in the state of grace. For this reason it is customary to receive the sacrament of Penance first unless one is unconscious. (1517)

Can this sacrament be received more than once?

Yes, the sacrament of the Anointing can be received more than once, even during the same illness if the sick person's condition worsens. This holds also for the elderly who gradually weaken. One should also receive it before a serious operation. (1515)

What are the last sacraments?

The last sacraments are those received by a person who is seriously ill. They include Penance, the Anointing of the Sick, and Viaticum (Holy Eucharist). Together these three are the sacraments for the final journey, for the end of our "earthly pilgrimage." (1517, 1525)

> *Whoever feeds on my flesh and drinks my blood has eternal life, and I will raise him up on the last day. . . .* (Jn 6:54)

How does one prepare when a priest is called for the Anointing of the Sick?

Cover a small table with a white cloth. If possible, the table should be prepared near the bed so as to be within sight of the sick person. Candles should be provided, as well as holy water where customary.

When the priest enters the house, he gives everyone a greeting of peace and then places the Blessed Sacrament on the table. If sacramental confession is not part of the rite, or if others are to receive Communion along with the sick person, the priest invites them to join in a penitential rite. A text from Scripture may then be read by one of those present or by the priest, who may then explain the text. The Lord's Prayer follows; then the priest distributes Holy Communion while a period of sacred silence is observed. A concluding prayer and a blessing complete the Rite of Communion of the Sick. The sacrament of the Anointing may be given at this time also.

At times deacons or Eucharistic ministers may visit the sick. Although they cannot celebrate the sacraments of Penance or Anointing, they can distribute Holy Communion.

Sacraments at the Service of Communion

Holy Orders

What is Holy Orders?

Holy Orders is the sacrament that continues Christ's mission through the grace and power given to men to carry out the sacred duties of deacons, priests, or bishops. (1536)

Why is this sacrament called "Orders"?

The word "Orders" derives from a term used in ancient Rome to refer to a specific group of persons, such as a governing body. Members are ordained, or incorporated into this body; they enter the order. (1537–1538)

You are a priest forever, in the line of Melchizedek. (Heb 5:6)

Is this priesthood the same as that which God established among the Chosen People?

No, the hereditary priesthood of Israel was the special mission of the house of Levi, which offered prayers and sacrifices for sin in the name of the whole people. The Church sees in this ancient priesthood a prefiguring of the New Testament priesthood which continues to offer the one redemptive sacrifice of Christ. (1539–1543)

Now since the Torah has but a shadow of the good things to come rather than their exact likeness, the same sacrifices which are offered

year after year can never perfect those who draw near to wor-
ship. . . . Therefore, when Christ came into the world he said,
"Sacrifice and offering you did not desire, but you have prepared a
body for me." (Heb 10:1, 5)

What is the relationship between the ministerial priest-hood and the priesthood of the faithful?

Both the priesthood of the faithful and the ministerial priesthood participate in the one priesthood of Christ. The priesthood of the faithful is an unfolding of the grace of Baptism, of faith, hope, and charity, of life in the Spirit. The ministerial priesthood, instead, is one of service to the common priesthood of the faithful. Because it is the means Christ uses to make his salvific graces available to the whole Church, the ministerial priesthood is itself conferred by a sacrament. (1546–1547)

Like living stones let yourselves be built up into a spiritual house,
a holy priesthood to offer spiritual sacrifices which are acceptable to
God through Jesus Christ. (1 Pt 2:5)

Does the priest act for Christ?

In his official capacity as an ordained minister, the priest acts in the person of Christ, the Head of the Church. The priest represents Christ, who acts as priest, teacher, and shepherd through him. (1548–1549)

If Christ acts through the priest, what of the priest's human weaknesses and sins?

The guarantee that Christ acts through the ordained minister extends only to the sacramental ministry, which is protected even against the priest's personal unworthiness. The priest will still put his own human stamp on his actions. He can, however, "put on" Christ's likeness more and more by his practice of prayer, penance, and virtue. (1550)

What is the proper reaction to scandalous behavior by the clergy?

While we will naturally be appalled by scandalous behavior, particularly pedophilia, by a priest or other minister of the Church, we remember to pray for the perpetrator as well as the victim because both are God's children. Keeping this truth in mind will help us sustain our trust in God and his Church despite the hurt and scandal.

What are the three degrees of the sacrament of Orders?

The episcopate, presbyterate, and diaconate comprise the three degrees of this sacrament. The episcopate (the office of a bishop) is the fullness of the sacrament. (1554)

Why is episcopal ordination the fullness of the sacrament of Holy Orders?

Episcopal ordination confers the fullest participation in the priesthood of Christ. The bishops are successors of the apostles and continue their ministry of teaching, shepherding, and leading the flock of Jesus Christ to holiness. In a special way they represent Christ as teacher, shepherd, and priest. (1555–1558)

What is the college of bishops?

Although each bishop is consecrated as pastor in a local Church, he is, together with all the other bishops, responsible for all the Churches. The practice of having several bishops take part in the consecration of a new bishop shows this collegiality. Each new bishop must be approved by the Pope who is the sign of the communion and universality of the one Church, as well as guarantor of the freedom of the particular Churches. (1559–1560)

What is the mission of the priest?

Priests are coworkers of the bishops and, like them, share in Christ's office of teacher, shepherd, and priest. Priests are to preach the Gospel, exercise the pastoral ministry, and lead the faithful in worship. A special part of their sacramental ministry is offering the Eucharist and acting for Christ in the sacrament of Penance. (1562–1566)

> *For every high priest is chosen from among men and appointed to represent them before God, to offer gifts and sacrifices for their sins.* (Heb 5:1)

What is the role of deacons?

Deacons are ordained by the bishop to the ministry of service. They assist the bishop and priests by baptizing, proclaiming God's Word to the faithful, preaching, distributing Communion, giving Eucharistic Benediction, blessing couples who receive the sacrament of Matrimony, presiding over funerals, and performing many works of service. (1569–1570)

> *For even the Son of Man came, not to be served, but to serve, and to give his life as a ransom for many.* (Mk 10:45)

How many kinds of deacons are there?

Permanent deacons are single or married men who will remain deacons for the rest of their lives. Transitional deacons are men who are ordained to the diaconate before being ordained as priests.

Who can confer Holy Orders?

The bishop confers Holy Orders. He places his hands on the head of the one to be ordained, praying that the Holy Spirit will consecrate him and give him the gifts proper to his ministry. The sign of the sacrament consists in this. Each degree of ordination confers an "indelible spiritual character." (1573–1574, 1581–1583)

> *For this reason I remind you to stir up the flame of God's gift, which is yours through the laying on of my hands.* . . . (2 Tm 1:6)

Who may receive Holy Orders?

A man who is a good Catholic, has prepared himself by study, and has been accepted by the bishop may receive Holy Orders. (1577–1578, 1580)

Does anyone have a right to be ordained?

No one has a right to be ordained, for a man is called to the priesthood by God through the Church. Ordination is God's gift, not a right. (1578)

Why are women not ordained to the priesthood?

In fidelity to the example of Jesus, the Church does not consider itself authorized to ordain women. The constant practice and tradition of the Church, from the earliest times, has been to ordain only men. (1577)

Why don't priests of the Latin rite marry?

Priests of the Latin rite observe celibacy for the sake of the kingdom of heaven that they may serve Christ with an undivided heart, dedicate themselves more freely and completely to their priestly ministry, and become living signs of the world to come. (1579)

Do some Catholic priests marry?

Some priests of the Eastern rite Catholic Churches marry, in accord with their ancient traditions, which have the approval of Rome. However, they must be married before their ordination. Also, some married Episcopalian or Anglican priests who have converted to Catholicism have been ordained as Catholic priests. (1580)

Does the Church have the right to require priestly celibacy?

The Church has the right to set up obligatory disciplinary norms which every seminarian studies; if the seminarian decides to become a priest, he freely and knowingly accepts the norm of celibacy.

What is the special grace given to those who receive the sacrament of Holy Orders?

The Holy Spirit confers a special grace that configures the one ordained to Christ as priest, teacher, and pastor. This grace makes the one ordained a minister of Christ. (1585–1588)

Matrimony

Who instituted marriage?

God instituted marriage by creating human beings, both male and female, in his own image which is love. Mutual love and procreation are essential aspects of the nature of man and woman. The Scriptural account of Genesis confirms this. (1602–1605)

> *It is not good that the man should be alone; I will make him a helper fit for him. Therefore a man leaves his father and his mother and cleaves to his wife, and they become one flesh.* (Gen 2:18, 24)

What is Matrimony?

Matrimony is the sacrament through which a baptized man and a baptized woman join themselves for life in a lawful marriage, which is a covenant of love and a "partnership of the whole of life." (1601)

How is marriage a covenant?

As an agreement to be faithful to one another for life, marriage is a covenant. It mirrors the nuptial covenant of God with Israel and of Christ with redeemed humanity. (1612, 1660, 1662)

What did Christ do for marriage?

Marriage has been taken up into the redemption Christ won for us. The Church sees in Christ's presence at the wedding in Cana his intention to sacramentalize marriage, that is, to make it "an efficacious sign" of his presence which "signifies and communicates grace." (1608, 1612–1613, 1617)

Jesus also was invited to the wedding. . . . (Jn 2:1–11)

What is the purpose of Matrimony?

The purpose of Matrimony is twofold: the mutual love and communion of husband and wife, and the generation and proper upbringing of children. These two purposes—the giving of life and the giving of love—are inseparable. (1601, 1660)

Husbands, love your wives, just as Christ loved the Church and gave himself up for her. . . . I am applying it to Christ and the Church, but each one of you should in the same way love his wife as he loves himself, and the wife should respect her husband. . . . Raise [your children] by instructing and admonishing them as the Lord would. (Eph 5:25, 32–33; 6:4)

Does Christian marriage have yet another dimension?

Christian marriage is a sacred sign recalling the perpetual love of Christ and his Church. Christ strengthens the union of the married couple through the special sacramental grace of Matrimony, which helps them become holy through their married life. (1617, 1641–1642)

How are consecrated virginity and marriage related?

Consecrated virginity and marriage are both gifts of God. They are complementary and inseparable signs of his love. (1618–1620)

> *So, then, they are no longer two but instead are one flesh. . . . Some who are eunuchs make themselves eunuchs for the sake of the kingdom of heaven.* (Mt 19:6, 12)

When does a Catholic receive the sacrament of Matrimony?

A Catholic receives the sacrament of Matrimony when he or she marries in the Church or with the Church's permission. (1621, 1623)

What is necessary to receive the sacrament of Matrimony worthily?

To receive the sacrament of Matrimony worthily it is necessary to be free from serious sin, to know and understand the duties of married life, and to obey the laws of the Church concerning marriage. (1622)

Why is it encouraged to wed at a nuptial Mass?

Couples are encouraged to wed at a nuptial Mass, rather than simply at the nuptial ceremony, so that they will seal their mutual self-offering within the celebration of Christ's self-offering for the Church. By receiving Communion they receive the Body and Blood of Christ and truly form "one body" in the Lord. (1621)

The bread we break, is it not a sharing in Christ's body? Because there is one bread, we who are many are one body. (1 Cor 10:16–17)

What is the "sign" of Matrimony?

The sign of Matrimony is the exchange of vows to love and be loyal to one another for a lifetime. "This consent that binds the spouses to each other finds its fulfillment in the two 'becoming one flesh'" (1627).

How is Matrimony given?

The indispensable aspect of Matrimony is the free and lawful exchange of consent. The man and woman give and accept one another for the purpose of establishing a marriage: "I take you to be my husband (wife)." The term "marriage vows" is popularly used to emphasize the solemnity of the covenant. This exchange of vows is sealed by the Holy Spirit's blessing upon the new covenant of love. (1623–1627)

For this reason a man shall leave his father and mother and be joined to his wife, and the two shall be one flesh. This is a tremendous mystery. (Eph 5:31–32)

Who acts for Jesus in Matrimony?

In the Latin Church the man and woman who are receiving Matrimony give the sacrament to each other. The priest or deacon witnesses the sacrament and gives the couple God's blessing. In the Eastern rites the priest is the minister of the sacrament. (1623, 1626–1630)

Who may receive the sacrament of Matrimony?

To receive the sacrament of Matrimony a person must be baptized, freely consent, and not already be married. The person must follow the marriage laws of the Church. (1625)

How should Catholics prepare for marriage?

Preparation for marriage starts in the home, where children can see Christian marriage lived out through the example of their parents, even when difficulties and problems arise. Later, suitable instruction about marriage, living a good Christian life, prayer, and receiving the sacraments can help the young person prepare for marriage. (1632)

Why does the Church make laws regulating marriage?

The Church makes laws regarding the marriages of Catholics because she has authority from Christ over all the sacraments and other spiritual matters that affect baptized persons. (1631)

May a person receive the sacrament of Matrimony more than once?

After the death of one's spouse, a person is free to receive Matrimony again.

A woman is bound as long as her husband is alive, but if her husband dies she is free to marry whoever she wishes to, as long as he is in the Lord. (1 Cor 7:39)

How do we know that people are free to marry?

The conference of bishops determines what inquiries should be made to determine that nothing stands in the way of true marriage. The priest will interview the couple about the appropriate laws. (1625)

What are impediments to marriage?

Impediments are obstacles that prevent a marriage from lawfully taking place and/or can make it invalid, such as underage, an existing valid marriage, sacred Orders, or close blood relationship. (1625)

Can there be dispensations from these impediments?

The Church can grant a dispensation from some of these impediments, but not from all of them.

If an invalid marriage was contracted, can it be remedied?

Even if the couple was unaware of the impediment, their marriage is invalid. In many cases, however, this situation can be remedied. A priest should be consulted and, if necessary, a dispensation obtained from the bishop. Then the marriage can be rectified, or "blessed."

What is an annulment?

A decree of nullity or annulment is a decision by Church authorities that an apparently valid marriage can be declared null because of a fatal flaw. These flaws, unknown to one or both parties, or concealed by one or the other, make the marriage no marriage from the start. Church "tribunals" study each case and, where proper, declare the annulment. (1629)

Does a decree of nullity make the children illegitimate?

No, the children who were conceived or born before the marriage was found to be null are legitimate children of a putative marriage—that is, of a marriage that was thought to exist.

What is a mixed marriage?

A mixed marriage is the marriage of a Catholic to a baptized non-Catholic. (1633)

What is a marriage with disparity of cult?

A marriage with disparity of cult is the marriage of a Catholic and a non-baptized person. (1633)

Does the Church permit these marriages?

Yes, but mixed marriages require ecclesiastical permission, and marriages with disparity of cult require a dispensation. Catholics who enter such marriages must take great care to strengthen their faith, give good example, and raise their children as Catholics. (1635)

Why does the Church encourage Catholics to marry other Catholics?

The union of husband and wife in Matrimony is a sign of Christ's union with the Church. Married partners are called to a union of mind and communion of life, and this union is fostered by unity of faith. Although the lives of many couples show a wonderful unity despite religious differences, these differences can cause difficulties at times. (1634–1637)

What are the effects of the sacrament of Matrimony?

It creates a permanent, irrevocable bond and confers on the couple the special grace of this sacrament. This grace, which comes from Christ, strengthens spouses to love each other and be faithful for life, to grow in holiness, and to welcome and educate their children. (1638–1641)

What are the requirements of conjugal love?

Because conjugal love involves such a deep union, it calls for the lifelong fidelity of the spouses to each other in an unbreakable union, and an openness to the gift of children. (1643)

Why is the marriage bond unbreakable?

Because marriage is a covenant, it calls for a total commitment, not a temporary one. We know that God wills the marriage bond to be unbreakable because Jesus confirmed it in a discussion on divorce. The "unbreakableness" of marriage, called indissolubility, is for the good of the couple, their children, and of society. (1614–1616, 1640, 1643–1646)

> *Have you not read that from the beginning the Creator made them male and female? And he said, "For this reason a man shall leave father and mother and be united with his wife, and the two shall become one flesh." So, then, they are no longer two but one flesh. Therefore, what God has joined together, let man not separate.* (Mt 19:4–6)

Does the Church ever permit a separation?

For a good reason, the Church allows the partners of a valid marriage a separation, but without the right to marry again. (1649)

What are some reasons the Church permits separation?

Some reasons are adultery of one of the spouses, criminal or abusive conduct, violence, danger to the spouse or children, or other serious reasons. Because the couple remain husband and wife despite the separation and are not free to remarry, it would be good to work out a reconciliation if that is possible and wise. However, no one is required to stay in an abusive situation. (1649)

> *Those who are married, I command you—not I, but the Lord—a wife shall not separate from her husband, but if she does separate, she must either remain unmarried or be reconciled with her husband, nor should a husband leave his wife.* (1 Cor 7:10–11)

What is divorce?

Divorce is an attempt to dissolve through civil law a marriage bond that can never be broken, except by death. (1650)

> *They said, "Moses permitted a husband to write a bill of divorce and put his wife away." Jesus said to them, "He wrote that*

commandment for you because of the hardness of your heart. But from the beginning of creation he made them male and female; for this reason a man shall leave his father and mother and be united with his wife and the two shall become one flesh. So, then, they are no longer two but one flesh. Therefore, what God has joined together, let man not separate." (Mk 10:4–9)

Is divorce ever permitted?

Divorce with remarriage is never permitted by the Church. The Church might permit a couple to obtain a civil divorce for legal reasons, but in God's eyes the couple is only separated. Neither may marry again while his or her spouse is still living. (1664)

> *Anyone who puts his wife away and marries another commits adultery, and whoever marries a woman put away by her husband commits adultery.* (Lk 16:18)

What are some needs of divorced Catholics who have not remarried?

Divorced Catholics who have not remarried need appropriate and compassionate pastoral care, encouragement to keep close to the sacraments, especially Holy Communion, and encouragement to not enter an invalid marriage, which would deprive them from receiving the life-giving and life-sustaining sacraments. (1649)

What are some needs of Catholics living in an invalid marriage?

Catholics living in an invalid marriage have particular pastoral needs. The *Catechism of the Catholic Church* states: ". . . priests and the whole community must manifest an attentive solicitude, so that they do not consider themselves separated from the Church, in whose life they can and must participate as baptized persons." (1651)

May Catholics remarried after divorce receive the sacraments?

Catholics who have remarried after a divorce (without having obtained an annulment) may not receive the Eucharist nor the sacrament of Penance unless they are "committed to living in complete continence." (1650, 1665)

How are adultery and polygamy sins against marriage?

Adultery, which is sexual intercourse between a married person and someone who is not his or her spouse, and polygamy, which is taking more than one spouse, are both sins against the undivided and exclusive nature of conjugal love. (1645)

How are children a blessing to a married couple?

Children are a living reflection of a couple's love, a permanent sign of their unity, and a living synthesis of their fatherhood and motherhood. (1652)

Is marriage rendered invalid by childlessness?

A valid marriage is not rendered invalid by unforeseen circumstances. If a couple married with the intention of accepting the children God would send them, childlessness does not render the marriage invalid. Their fruitfulness can be expressed in other ways, perhaps by providing a loving home for an adopted child, or by offering hospitality to others, or by works of charity, sacrifice, and service. (1654)

Are Catholic couples obliged to have as many children as possible?

No, Catholic couples are obliged only to act in a truly responsible manner in bringing children into the world and raising them well. This responsibility includes recognizing the procreation of children as one of the fundamental purposes of marriage and avoiding abortion and contraception, as well as genetic manipulation, as contrary to God's law.

Is there an acceptable method of regulating births?

The Church recognizes natural methods for the regulation of births because these do not directly block God's creative action (as opposed to contraception; for more on this see pages 215–216). Just reasons may exist for the couple to practice responsible parenthood by spacing the births of their children. The Church recommends that the couple obtain information about natural methods from Catholic natural family planning groups. (2366–2368)

Why is the family called the domestic church?

The Christian family is the "domestic church," a unique and irreplaceable community of persons that is like the Church in miniature. All the members are called to holiness in fulfilling their duties and in their relationship as a family. They are meant to be a leaven in society, a sign of God's presence in the world. The family is the first school of faith, virtue, and prayer. This does not mean that family life will be without difficulties, but that Jesus will always be present to help families face any problems that may arise. (1655–1658)

Sacramentals

What are sacramentals?

Sacramentals are "sacred signs which bear a resemblance to the sacraments. They signify effects, particularly of a spiritual nature, which are obtained through the intercession of the Church." They can dispose us to receive the chief effects of the sacraments, and to make holy various occasions in life. (1667–1668)

Where does the name "sacramental" come from?

The sacramentals are so named because many of them are used in the celebration of the sacraments, and they, too, like the sacraments, are external signs through which blessings are received from God.

How does a sacramental obtain blessings from God?

A sacramental obtains blessings from God through the Paschal Mystery of Christ, by the prayers that the Church offers for those using the sacramental, and because of the devotion that the object, action, or word inspires. (1670)

Which blessings are obtained through sacramentals?

Through sacramentals we can obtain God's graces and blessings, the forgiveness of venial sins, spiritual strength and comfort, and sometimes health and other material blessings, if this is according to God's will.

How are sacramentals different from sacraments?

Sacramentals are instituted by the Church, while the sacraments were instituted by Christ. Sacramentals obtain grace through the prayers of the Church and depend on the faith and good dispositions of the person using them. The sacraments, instead, operate by the direct power of Christ. (1670)

Why did the Church institute sacramentals?

The Church instituted sacramentals to add more dignity to the ritual of the sacraments, to help us to participate more fully in the liturgy and the sacraments, and to make holy various occasions in life.

What is the basis for sacramentals?

The basis for sacramentals is our own Baptism by which we receive the baptismal priesthood. God calls us to be a "blessing" and to bless. (1669)

Respond with blessings for this is your calling and in this way you will obtain a blessing. (1 Pt 3:9)

What are the principal sacramentals?

The principal sacramentals are the liturgical year and the public prayer of the Church, the Liturgy of the Hours.

What are some other types of sacramentals?

Some other types of sacramentals are:
- ❖ the blessing of persons, places, and objects;
- ❖ blessings that consecrate persons to God or reserve places and objects for liturgical use, such as religious profession or the consecration of an altar;
- ❖ exorcisms for the removal of evil spirits. (1669, 1671–1674)

*And to whatever house you enter, first say, "Peace be to this house."
If there is a son of peace there your peace will rest upon him.* (Lk
10:5–6)

What are some actions that are sacramentals?

Some actions that are sacramentals are genuflecting, kneeling, bowing the head, making the sign of the cross, folding the hands, sprinkling with holy water.

So Moses made a bronze serpent, and set it on a pole; and if a serpent bit any man, he would look at the bronze serpent and live.
(Num 21:9)

Which blessed objects of popular devotion do Catholics commonly use?

Rosaries, relics, medals, crucifixes, scapulars, ashes, palms, candles, and depictions of Jesus, Mary, and the saints are popular objects of devotion. (1674)

Do blessed objects bring good luck?

Blessed objects should never be considered good luck charms, nor made the objects of superstition. For example, one cannot lead an immoral life and think that merely wearing the scapular or medal without true repentance will obtain the grace of conversion before death.

What is a scapular?

A scapular consists of two small pieces of cloth, fastened by strings and worn around the neck in front and in back in imitation of the part of a religious habit called the scapular. Scapulars that are worn around the neck are a sign of association in the spirituality of a particular religious order. The most common scapular honors Mary as Our Lady of Mount Carmel. A scapular medal may be worn in place of a cloth scapular.

What is holy water?

Holy water, or water blessed by a priest, is a sacramental that reminds us of our Baptism and our commitment to live the Christian life. It is usually found in the entrance of a church, and we make the sign of the cross with it upon entering and leaving church. (1668)

What is the purpose of blessed candles?

Blessed candles are lit to witness to our devotion to Jesus who is light and life with his grace.

What is the purpose of blessed ashes?

Blessed ashes are used especially on Ash Wednesday, the first day of Lent. A cross is traced with ashes on our forehead as a reminder to live a good life and do penance because one day we will die.

What is the purpose of crucifixes, medals, scapulars, religious statues, and holy pictures?

These objects remind us of Jesus and also our union with the saints, and call us to lead lives of prayer and Christian service.

Do we pray to religious statues and pictures?

We do not pray to the religious statues and pictures themselves. Instead, we honor the persons in heaven whom the statues and depictions represent, and ask these persons' intercession for us.

What are rosary beads?

They are "prayer beads" used to pray the Rosary. This "Gospel prayer" is made up of the Our Father, Hail Mary, and Glory, in which we think about important events in the lives of Jesus and Mary. (See pages 261–262 for instructions on how to pray the Rosary.)

LIFE IN CHRIST

The Dignity of the Human Person

How is the human person the image and likeness of God?

In his or her spiritual soul, intellect, and free will, the human person is the image and likeness of God. Our whole being is ordered to seeking truth and goodness in accord with our destiny, which is eternal blessedness with God. *Moreover, as persons we are called to be in communion through love with other human beings, and this reflects in some way the communion of Persons in the Blessed Trinity.* (1701–1704)

> *Then God said, "Let us make man in our image, after our likeness."* (Gen 1:26)

How is the body also God's image?

God's image is also seen in the human body in its ability to create new life through love and bestow love on others through its members.

What is the theology of the body?

Among Catholics, the term "theology of the body" generally refers to the series of addresses given by Pope John Paul II concerning the embodied nature of the human person. In his extensive catechesis, the Pope developed the concept that the body reveals the person, and he explored what this means in human life, love, sexuality, and relationships, especially for marriage and celibacy.

How do we seek eternal blessedness?

We seek to reach eternal blessedness with God by following the dictates of our conscience to do good and avoid evil. This is lived out in our daily efforts to love God and neighbor. (1706)

Why is it such a struggle to be good?

Despite our makeup and destiny, our life is a continual struggle because original sin wounded our nature, leaving us attracted to sin. (1707)

> *For the flesh's desires are opposed to the Spirit, and the Spirit is opposed to the flesh. They are opposed to each other so you will not just do whatever you want.* (Gal 5:17)

What is the new life in Christ?

By his passion, death, and resurrection Jesus merited a new life for us. He restored to us what was lost by sin and renews us by grace in the Holy Spirit. (1708–1709)

> *Thus, you too should consider yourselves dead to sin and living for God in Christ Jesus.* (Rom 6:11)

Who is a Christian?

A Christian is a baptized follower of Jesus Christ. (1694)

> *Be imitators of me, just as I imitate Christ.* (1 Cor 11:1)

What is Christian morality?

Christian morality is living in a way worthy of our dignity as human beings and God's adopted children.

> *He who called you is holy, and so you too should be holy in all your conduct, since it is written, "You shall be holy because I am holy."* (1 Pt 1:15–16)

What great commandment is to be lived by all who believe in God?

The great commandment to be lived by all who believe in God is to love God. (2055)

"You shall love the Lord with all your heart and with all your soul and with all your understanding"; this is the first and greatest commandment. And the second is like it, "You shall love your neighbor as yourself." (Mt 22:37–39)

What does Jesus's commandment of love mean for us?

We are to love God with our whole being and to love others as Jesus loves us, because God loves them and wants us to do the same. The spiritual and corporal works of mercy are ways to show this love. (See also Dt 6:4ff.) (1972)

What are the works of mercy?

Based on Matthew 25:35–36, the corporal works of mercy are to feed the hungry, to give drink to the thirsty, to clothe the naked, to shelter the homeless, to visit the sick, to visit the imprisoned, and to bury the dead. (2447)

What are the spiritual works of mercy?

The spiritual works of mercy are to counsel the doubtful, to instruct the ignorant, to admonish the sinner, to comfort the sorrowful, to forgive injuries, to bear wrongs patiently, and to pray for the living and the dead. (2447)

What are the Beatitudes?

The Beatitudes are the core of Jesus's teaching. They describe both our attitude as disciples of Christ and the promises of the kingdom. (1716–1717)

Blessed are the poor in spirit, for theirs is the kingdom of heaven.
Blessed are those who mourn, for they shall be comforted.
Blessed are the meek, for they shall inherit the earth.
Blessed are those who hunger and thirst to do God's will,
for they shall have their fill.
Blessed are the merciful, for they shall receive mercy.
Blessed are the pure of heart, for they shall see God.
Blessed are the peacemakers, for they shall be called sons of God.
Blessed are those who are persecuted for doing God's will, for
theirs is the kingdom of heaven.

Blessed are you when they insult you and persecute you and say
every sort of evil thing against you on account of me; rejoice and be
glad, because your reward will be great in heaven—they perse-
cuted the prophets before you in the same way. (Mt 5:3–12)

Are the Beatitudes truly practical?

The Beatitudes are practical in that they offer us concrete ways to conform our life to the life and teachings of Christ. Just as the commandments express our desire for the true and good, so the Beatitudes express our natural desire for happiness. By living the Beatitudes we can begin to experience the life to come. (1717–1719)

He has bestowed on us the great and precious promises, so that
through them you may escape from the corruption that passion
brought into the world and may come to share in the divine nature.
(2 Pt 1:4)

What is the challenge of the Beatitudes?

The Beatitudes challenge us to conform all our choices to the teachings of Jesus Christ. Living as his disciples should be our one true concern and the guiding principle in all our actions. (1723–1724)

Lead me in your truth, and teach me, for you are the God of my
salvation; for you I wait all day long. (Ps 25:5)

What is human freedom?

Human freedom is our ability "to initiate and control" our own actions. We choose to do or not to do each action and are responsible for what we have chosen. Freedom does not mean simply doing what we want, but being free to choose the good. (1730–1731)

> *It was [the Lord] who created humankind in the beginning, and he left them in the power of their own free choice. f you choose, you can keep the commandments, and to act faithfully is a matter of your own choice.* (Sir 15:14–15)

Does grace interfere with our freedom?

No. When we sin we weaken our freedom and become slaves of our desires, but when we rely on grace, our inner freedom is strengthened and enhanced. (1740–1742)

> *Where the Spirit of the Lord is, there is freedom.* (2 Cor 3:17)

How do we judge the morality of an act?

We judge the morality of an act by asking:
- ❖ Is the action good or evil in itself?
- ❖ What is our intention or end in choosing it?
- ❖ What are the circumstances or consequences of this action?

For an act to be morally good, all three aspects must be good. For example, an act that is evil in itself, such as murder, cannot be made right by a good intention, such as relieving suffering. (1749–1756)

> *He who walks in integrity walks securely.* (Prov 10:9)

What are the passions?

Passions are the feelings or emotions we experience, which are neither good nor evil in themselves. Their moral value depends on the way they are used by the mind and will. (1762–1770)

> *Those who belong to Christ have crucified the flesh with its passions and desires.* (Gal 5:24)

What are the principal passions?

The *Catechism of the Catholic Church* lists the principal passions as "love and hatred, desire and fear, joy, sadness, and anger." (1772)

Conscience

What is conscience?

Conscience is a practical judgment (decision) as to whether an action, word, thought, desire, or omission is good and to be consented to, or evil and to be avoided. It is our most secret core and sanctuary where we are alone with God. (1776–1778)

> They show that what the Torah requires is written on their hearts. Their consciences also bear witness, their conflicting thoughts accusing or even defending them on the day when, according to my gospel, God judges men's secrets through Christ Jesus. (Rom 2:15–16)

Must we follow our conscience?

If we have reflected well and are certain that something is the right thing to do, we must follow our conscience. (1778)

What is necessary to have a correct conscience?

To have a correct conscience, one first needs to know God's law (as it is known in the natural law and revealed in the Bible), the laws of the Church, and the particular duties of one's state in life. Then one's conscience will better express what is right or wrong in a particular situation. In addition, one needs to be prudent and upright in order to apply these criteria to the matter at hand. (1783)

What role do others play in our formation of conscience?

Among those who help in the formation of conscience, parents play the major role by the instruction, example, and guidance they give to their children. They are the first and the constant teachers of their children, instructing them about God's love and his law, the duties of religion and society, virtues and family values. Others who influence the formation of conscience are pastors, teachers, relatives, and civil and religious authorities. (1784)

Does prayer influence conscience?

Yes, prayer enlightens and strengthens conscience, giving it the direction of God's Word. We need to examine our intentions and actions in the light of prayer. The grace of the Holy Spirit helps us to recognize and choose what is God's will. (1785)

Are we responsible for our actions?

We are truly responsible for our actions because God gave us an intellect and free will, which we are to use to fulfill the purpose for which he made us. (1730)

The righteousness of the righteous shall be upon himself, and the wickedness of the wicked shall be upon himself. (Ezek 18:20)

Can we act with a doubtful conscience?

A doubtful conscience is one which cannot decide if an act is good and to be done, or evil and to be avoided. When in such a doubt, one must either refrain from acting or resolve the doubt. (1787)

What is a scrupulous conscience?

A scrupulous conscience is one that is constantly in doubt, in fear of sin when there is none, or in fear of mortal sin when there is only venial sin. A scrupulous conscience can be helped by direction from a wise confessor, humble prayer, and sometimes by professional help.

What is a lax conscience?

A lax conscience is one which judges more by convenience than by God's law and leads a person to easily commit sin, slight or serious. Everything is judged carelessly, without thought of the consequences or the offense to God. (1791)

If a conscience errs because of invincible ignorance, does the person sin?

No, if a conscience errs because of invincible (unavoidable) ignorance, the person does not sin. We should make efforts, however, to learn so that we have a correctly formed conscience. (1793)

> *Their understanding is clouded and they are alienated from God's life because of their ignorance. . . .* (Eph 4:18)

Is everything that is legal, morally right?

Everything that is legal is not necessarily morally right. Civil law cannot contradict the law of God. For example, the legality of abortion does not make it morally right. (1782)

> *We have to obey God rather than men.* (Acts 5:29)

Does a good end ever justify the use of evil means?

No, we are never permitted to do evil in order that good may result from it. God wants us to have a good end and reach it by doing good deeds. Anyone, especially a Christian, must be ready to make sacrifices, and if necessary, even to go to death for the sake of one's salvation. (1789)

What if "everyone else is doing it"?

"Everyone else is doing it" cannot excuse our wrongdoing, since God's law is not based on popularity, but on his divine will and our final end.

I urge you to watch out for those who cause dissension and raise obstacles which are contrary to what you were taught. (Rom 16:17)

Virtue

What is virtue?

Virtue is a power to do good or a habit of doing good. The main virtues are the theological (God-centered) virtues and the cardinal (hinge or key) virtues. Although these powers are free gifts of God, we must use them so that they truly become the habits of doing good that God meant them to be. (1803)

> *Whatever is true, whatever is honorable, whatever is just, whatever is pure, whatever is pleasing, whatever is gracious, if there is any excellence or anything praiseworthy, think of these things.* (Phil 4:8)

What are moral virtues?

The moral virtues are human virtues or dispositions, attitudes and habits of conducting oneself in an upright and orderly way. They are strengths of character developed by personal effort that enable a person to live with freedom and self-control. (1804)

> *You should make every effort to supplement your faith with virtue, your virtue with knowledge, your knowledge with self-control, your self-control with steadfastness, your steadfastness with godliness, your godliness with mutual affection, and your mutual affection with love.* (2 Pt 1:5–7)

What are the cardinal virtues?

The cardinal virtues are the key moral virtues: prudence, justice, fortitude, and temperance. The word "cardinal" comes from the Latin word for "hinge." The other moral virtues hinge on these four. (1805)

> *And if one loves righteousness, her labors are virtues; for she teaches self-control and prudence, justice and courage; nothing in life is more profitable . . . than these.* (Wis 8:7)

What is prudence?

Prudence is the virtue that enables us to think carefully before acting, to make wise choices, and to do things well. (1806)

> *The wisdom of a prudent man is to discern his way.* (Prov 14:8)

What is the virtue of justice?

Justice is the virtue that enables us to give God and neighbor their due, thus safeguarding the rights of God and others. (1807)

> *Then render to Caesar the things that are Caesar's and to God the things that are God's.* (Lk 20:25)

What is the virtue of fortitude?

Fortitude is the virtue by which we do what is good and right in spite of any difficulty. (1808)

> *You will have suffering in the world, but take courage! I have conquered the world!* (Jn 16:33)

What is the virtue of temperance?

Temperance is the virtue by which we exercise self-control with regard to the drives of human nature. (1809)

> *Reject impiety and worldly passions and . . . live sober, upright, and godly lives in this present age as we await our blessed hope. . . .* (Tit 2:12–13)

What are some other moral virtues?

Other moral virtues are:

❖ Religion, which helps us worship God worthily;

❖ Filial piety and patriotism, which help us love, honor, and respect our parents and nation;

❖ Obedience, which helps us obey our parents and all authorities who represent God;

❖ Truthfulness, which helps us always tell the truth;

❖ Liberality, which helps us use rightly the goods of this world;

❖ Patience, which helps us to face trials and difficulties with calmness;

❖ Humility, which helps us to know ourselves and be grateful for whatever is good in us;

❖ Chastity, or purity, which helps us to be pure in mind, heart, and body.

There are many other moral virtues besides these.

What are the theological virtues?

The theological virtues—faith, hope, and charity—have God as their origin, motive, and object. God gives them to us so that we might direct our whole life to him. (1812–1813)

So these three—faith, hope, and love—remain, but the greatest of them all is love. (1 Cor 13:13)

What does the word "theological" mean?

"Theological" means that which pertains to God.

What is the virtue of faith?

Faith is the supernatural virtue by which we believe all that God has revealed and teaches us through the Catholic Church, because he cannot deceive or be deceived. By faith we commit our whole selves to God. (1814)

God reveals his saving righteousness, from faith to faith, as it is written, "Whoever is righteous by faith shall live." (Rom 1:17)

Can we be saved by faith alone?

We cannot be saved by faith alone; God requires that we give life to our belief through good works which spring from love. (1815)

Faith by itself is dead, unless it is manifested in works. (Jas 2:17)

Does faith require anything of us?

Besides living our faith and constantly studying it, we must openly profess our faith. (1816)

Whoever acknowledges me before men, I, too, will acknowledge him before my Father in heaven; but whoever denies me before men, I, too, will deny him before my Father in heaven. (Mt 10:32–33)

How can we grow in our faith?

We can grow in our faith by making frequent acts of faith, by praying for an increase of faith, by studying the truths of faith, by living according to God's will, by choosing friends and associates wisely, and by reading or viewing only good things, avoiding anything against the teachings of the Church.

Be watchful, stand firm in the faith. . . . (1 Cor 16:13)

How do we put our faith into action?

We put our faith into action by bringing the Gospel spirit into every aspect of our lives, especially in our relations with others. We thus witness to Christ, extend the kingdom of God and build a more human world.

Always be ready with a reply for anyone who demands an expla-
nation for the hope you have within you, but do it humbly and
respectfully. . . . (1 Pt 3:15–16)

What is the virtue of hope?

Hope is the supernatural virtue by which we trust that God
will give us eternal life and all we need to obtain it, because he
is merciful and faithful to his promises. (1817)

Let us hold fast to the profession of our hope without wavering, for
the one who made the promise to us is faithful. (Heb 10:23)

How do we live by hope?

We live by hope by trusting that God will give us the graces
necessary for salvation and fulfill our desire for the blessedness
of the kingdom. (1818)

We even rejoice in our afflictions, since we know that affliction
produces steadfastness, steadfastness produces proven character, and
proven character produces hope. And this hope is no illusion, because
God's love has been poured out in our hearts through the Holy Spirit
which has been given to us. (Rom 5:3–5)

What is the virtue of charity?

Charity is the supernatural virtue by which we love God
above all, and love all other people as ourselves for the love of
God. (1822)

God is love, and whoever abides in love abides in God, and God
abides in him. . . . Whoever loves God must also love his brother.
(1 Jn 4:16, 21)

How do we live by charity?

We live by charity by living the two great commandments:
that is, loving God with all our heart, soul, mind, and strength,
because he is worthy of all our love; and by loving our neighbor

as ourselves for the love of God. In practice this involves obeying the commandments of God and of the Church and performing the works of mercy. (1823–1827)

> *Love is patient, love is kind, it is not jealous, does not boast, is not arrogant. Love is not dishonorable, is not selfish, is not irritable, does not keep a record of past wrongs. Love does not rejoice at injustice but rejoices in the truth. Love endures all things; love has complete faith and steadfast hope; love bears with everything.* (1 Cor 13:4–7)

What are the gifts of the Holy Spirit?

The gifts of the Holy Spirit are wisdom, understanding, counsel, fortitude, knowledge, piety, and fear of the Lord. These gifts prepare us to receive grace and make it easier to practice the virtues. They permanently dispose us to be receptive to the inspirations of the Holy Spirit. (1830–1831)

> *At the same time God bore witness through signs and wonders and all sorts of mighty deeds, and by distributing the gifts of the Holy Spirit according to his will.* (Heb 2:4)

What is the gift of wisdom?

The gift of wisdom helps us to love spiritual things, to put God first in our lives, and to judge what will be helpful and what will be an obstacle to reaching heaven.

What is the gift of understanding?

The gift of understanding helps us to see more deeply into the truths we already believe by faith.

What is the gift of counsel?

The gift of counsel or right judgment helps us to choose what is right, even in difficult circumstances.

What is the gift of fortitude?

The gift of fortitude or courage helps us to be brave and patient in overcoming difficulties and carrying out our duties.

What is the gift of knowledge?

The gift of knowledge helps us to evaluate created things in relation to God and to see them as instruments, not as goals.

What is the gift of piety?

The gift of piety helps us to love, reverence, and worship God as our Father, and to respect all people as our brothers and sisters, so that our service to both God and others will not be a burden.

What is the gift of fear of the Lord?

The gift of fear of the Lord helps us to respect God and to desire to please him in everything. It is not a fear of God, but a fear of offending him.

What are the fruits of the Holy Spirit?

The fruits of the Holy Spirit are perfections that result from our response to the Holy Spirit's impulses to do good (actual graces). The twelve fruits are charity, joy, peace, patience, kindness, goodness, generosity, gentleness, faithfulness, modesty, self-control, and chastity. (1832)

> *The Spirit's fruit is love, joy, peace, patience, kindness, goodness, faith, gentleness, self-control. There is no law against these things! If we live in the Spirit, let us also follow the Spirit!* (Gal 5:22–23, 25)

For what will God reward us?

God will reward us for all our victories over temptation and sin, for all our good deeds and sacrifices done out of love for him, and for all our efforts to grow closer to him.

Personal Sin

What is sin?

Sin is disobedience to God, an offense against him. It is also, as stated in the *Catechism of the Catholic Church*, "an offense against reason, truth, and right conscience; it is failure in genuine love for God and neighbor caused by a perverse attachment to certain goods." (1849–1850)

Everyone who commits sin is a slave of sin. (Jn 8:34)

What is actual sin?

Actual sin is the personal sin we commit. (1868)

Against you, you alone, have I sinned, and done what is evil in your sight . . . (Ps 51:4)

Are there different kinds of personal or actual sin?

There are two kinds of personal or actual sin: mortal and venial. (1854)

All wrongdoing is sinful, but there are some sins which are not mortal. (1 Jn 5:17)

What is mortal sin?

Mortal sin is a grave offense against God's law by which we prefer something created to the Creator. (1855)

Put to death those parts of you which are earthly—fornication, impurity, passion, evil desires, and that greed which is idolatry. (Col 3:5)

How can we know if a sin is mortal?

A sin is mortal or grave when these three conditions are present:

- ❖ grave matter, that is, a serious wrong or what is thought to be seriously wrong;
- ❖ full knowledge, that is, before or while committing it, the person clearly is aware that it is wrong;
- ❖ complete consent, that is, the person freely gives full consent to it. (1857–1859)

Can anything lessen or increase our responsibility for mortal sin?

Yes, responsibility for mortal sin can be lessened by "unintentional ignorance," passions, external pressures, and pathologies. Greater responsibility is imputed to anyone sinning through malice or hardness of heart, or to one who pretends not to know the seriousness of the sin. (See Lk 16:19–31.) (1859–1860)

What are the effects of mortal sin?

By mortal sin a person turns away from God and so loses the gift of charity and sanctifying grace. Mortal sin takes away the merit of the person's previous good actions and deprives one of the right to eternal happiness in heaven. Sincere repentance can reverse these effects. (1861)

Is God responsible for personal sin since God permits certain temptations?

God is not responsible for personal sin because he is all good and all holy, and for everyone who prays, God always provides sufficient grace to overcome temptations.

> Do not say, "It was the LORD's doing that I fell away"; for he does not do what he hates. Do not say, "It was he who led me astray." (Sir 15:11–12)

What is venial sin?

A sin is venial when one of the conditions for a mortal sin is missing. For example, the thought, desire, word, action, or omission is wrong but not seriously so, or it is seriously wrong but a person does not clearly see this, or does not fully consent to it. (1862)

What are the effects of venial sin?

Venial sin lessens our charity and weakens our practice of the Catholic faith. It makes us weaker when faced with temptations to serious sin, and hinders our spiritual growth. (1863)

Should we avoid venial sins?

Although they do not destroy the life of grace, we should avoid venial sins because they are an offense to God and weaken our friendship with him. They also turn our hearts away from God and toward some created good, which makes it easier to commit more serious sins. (1863)

What is a sin of omission?

A sin of omission is the failure to do something one should have done.

Are sins of omission mortal or venial?

Sins of omission may be mortal or venial depending upon what we have failed to do.

What are the chief reasons why people commit sin?

The chief reasons why people commit sin may be found in the seven capital sins. (1866)

What are the seven capital sins?

The seven capital sins are:
* ❖ pride—inordinate or uncontrolled self-esteem;
* ❖ avarice (or covetousness)—an excessive desire for created goods;
* ❖ envy—sorrow at another's good fortune;
* ❖ lust—uncontrolled sexual desire;
* ❖ wrath (or anger)—a strong, uncontrolled passion of displeasure;
* ❖ gluttony—excessive indulgence in food and/or drink;
* ❖ sloth—spiritual, mental, or physical laziness that causes one to neglect one's duties. (1866)

Draw near to God and he will draw near to you. (Jas 4:8)

What are the "sins that cry to heaven"?

The sins that cry to heaven are:

* ❖ voluntary murder;

The voice of your brother's blood is crying to me from the ground. (Gen 4:10)

* ❖ sodomy;

The outcry against Sodom and Gomorrah is great and their sin is grave. (Gen 18:20)

* ❖ taking advantage of the poor;

And now, behold, the cry of the people of Israel has come to me and I have seen the oppression with which the Egyptians oppress them. (Ex 3:9)

* ❖ oppression of foreigners, widows, and orphans;

You shall not wrong a stranger or oppress him, for you were strangers in the land of Egypt. You shall not afflict any widow or orphan. If you do afflict them, and they cry out to me, I will surely hear their cry. (Ex 22:21–23)

❖ injustice toward a worker. (1867)

Behold, the wages you withheld from the laborers who reaped your fields are crying out. (Jas 5:4)

What are the sins against the Holy Spirit?

The sins against the Holy Spirit are despair of one's salvation, presumption of saving oneself without merit or repentance, resisting the known truth, envy of the graces received by others, obstinacy in one's sins, and final impenitence. (1864)

Every sin and blasphemy will be forgiven you, but blasphemy against the Spirit will not be forgiven. (Mt 12:31)

What does it mean to say that blasphemy against the Spirit will not be forgiven?

God is infinitely merciful and ready to forgive any sin as long as we repent of it. Blasphemy against the Spirit is precisely a refusal to repent, by which the person rejects the grace that God offers.

What is an occasion of sin?

An occasion of sin is any circumstance (person, place, or thing) that leads one to sin.

Do we ever share responsibility for the sin of another?

Although sin is a personal act, we share in the responsibility for another person's sin if we cooperate with him or her in any of the following ways:

❖ by directly and freely taking part in the sin;
❖ by our advice, encouragement, or approval;
❖ by not reporting them or trying to stop them when we are obliged to;
❖ by protecting or hiding them. (1868)

Their hands are upon what is evil, to do it diligently: the prince and the judge ask for a bribe, and the great man utters the evil desire of his soul; thus they weave it together. (Mic 7:3)

What is social sin?

Social sin arises when people copy or cooperate with one another in allowing and promoting sin. This is often evident in what becomes socially acceptable or what is institutionalized in the social structure or laws. Some examples would be slavery, child labor, abortion, and neglect of the poor or marginalized. (1869)

What is the false theory called "situation ethics"?

Situation ethics teaches that there is no fixed moral code given to human beings by the Creator. It holds that individuals must make moral choices according to a particular situation— that is, what is right or best in this moment for me. The *Catechism of the Catholic Church* states: "There are acts which, in and of themselves, independently of circumstances and intentions, are always gravely illicit by reason of their object, such as blasphemy and perjury, murder and adultery." (1756)

What is the "fundamental option" theory?

The "fundamental option" theory teaches that a good person can do something considered gravely sinful, and yet that particular action is not gravely sinful for him or her. This is because the person's basic choice or fundamental option is for God and the good. The theory holds that one gravely sinful act (a mortal sin) is not enough to separate one from God; a series of gravely forbidden acts would be required to prove that one's option has changed. This teaching is false. It is not what the Church teaches regarding sin, free will, and personal responsibility for each of one's actions.

The Ten Commandments

What are the commandments of God?

The commandments of God are these ten: I am the Lord your God:

1. You shall not have other gods besides me.
2. You shall not take the name of the Lord your God in vain.
3. Remember to keep holy the Lord's day.
4. Honor your father and your mother.
5. You shall not kill.
6. You shall not commit adultery.
7. You shall not steal.
8. You shall not bear false witness against your neighbor.
9. You shall not covet your neighbor's wife.
10. You shall not covet your neighbor's goods. (See Ex 20:1–17.)

What is the origin of the Ten Commandments?

The Ten Commandments are introduced as the Decalogue ("ten words") in the Books of Exodus and Deuteronomy. The Lord gave them to Moses to bring to the people as the pledge of the covenant. (2056–2061)

The LORD our God made a covenant with us in Horeb. (Dt 5:2)

Are the Ten Commandments still relevant?

Yes. Jesus stressed their importance to his followers, for they express how we are to behave as God's children. Keeping them is our response to God's constant love for us. (2062, 2064–2068)

If you want to enter into life, keep the commandments. (Mt 19:17)

Is it acceptable to keep most, but not all of the commandments?

We cannot choose to observe only some of the command-ments. All of them are equally words of God, which he revealed to us for our good. They have a unity; to refuse to observe even one is to offend against all of them. (2069)

> *For whoever keeps the whole Torah but stumbles with regard to one commandment has become guilty of all of it.* (Jas 2:10)

Is it true that the Ten Commandments are written on our hearts?

Yes, the Ten Commandments are written on our hearts. They clearly state the rights and duties we have toward God and one another, which our consciences recognize naturally. (2070–2071)

Can the Ten Commandments of God be observed?

Even though the Ten Commandments involve serious obligations and we may face strong temptations against them, the grace to observe them is always available to the sincere of heart. (2072)

> *Walk according to the Spirit, and do not carry out the desires of the flesh.* (Gal 5:16)

How are the Ten Commandments divided?

The first three show us the way to love God; the other seven, how to love our neighbor.

What does St. Paul say about the Ten Commandments?

St. Paul says this:

> *See that you owe nothing, except for your obligation to love one another, for whoever loves his neighbor has fulfilled the Torah. . . .*

[The] commandments can be summed up in one sentence—you shall love your neighbor as yourself. (Rom 13:8–9)

How did Jesus sum up the Ten Commandments?

When asked which of the commandments was the most important, Jesus summed them up in these words:

"You shall love the Lord with all your heart and with all your soul and with all your understanding"; this is the first and greatest commandment. And the second is like it, "You shall love your neighbor as yourself." All the Torah and the prophets rests on these two commandments. (Mt 22:37–40)

First Commandment

What is the first commandment of God?

The first commandment of God is:

You shall have no other gods before me. (Dt 5:7) *You shall not go after other gods ... for the LORD your God in the midst of you is a jealous God.* (Dt 6:14–15)

What did Jesus say about the first commandment?

Jesus said:

For it is written, "The Lord your God shall you worship, and him alone shall you adore." (Mt 4:10)

What does the first commandment require of us?

The first commandment requires us to love God above all things, to serve him, and to adore him alone. To adore God means to worship him as our sovereign Creator and Lord, avoiding the sins of idolatry and sacrilege. (2096–2097)

You shall worship the Lord your God, and him only shall you serve. (Lk 4:8)

How do we practice our faith?

We exercise faith by believing in God and all he has revealed, and by witnessing to our belief by the way we live. A strong faith calls us to make the effort to develop and grow in it. (2087–2088)

Through him we have received the grace of apostleship to bring about the obedience of faith among all nations for the sake of his name. (Rom 1:5)

How can a Catholic sin against faith?

A Catholic sins against faith by joining a non-Catholic church, by denying a truth of faith, or by being indifferent to the Catholic religion. (2088–2089)

Fight the good fight with faith and a good conscience. By rejecting conscience certain persons have made a shipwreck of their faith. (1 Tm 1:18–19)

What is heresy?

Heresy is the deliberate denial of a truth of faith. (2089)

What is apostasy?

Apostasy is complete rejection of the Christian faith by a baptized Catholic. (2089)

What does it mean to hope?

We need God's grace to live good lives. We must confidently hope for his continued blessings until we enter his presence. (2090)

Be strong, and let your heart take courage, all you who wait for the LORD! (Ps 31:24)

How do we sin against hope?

We can sin against hope by presumption and despair.

Let us not grow tired of doing good, for in due time we will also reap a harvest if we do not give up. (Gal 6:9)

What is presumption?

Presumption is the sin of expecting that God will save us without any effort on our part, or presuming that we do not need God's help to reach heaven. (2092)

What you should say is, "If the Lord wills it we will live and we will do this or that," but in your arrogance you boast. (Jas 4:15–16)

What is despair?

Despair is the sin of refusing to believe that God will give one the necessary help to reach salvation. Despair is an act of the will, not to be confused with feelings of depression or anxiety. (2091)

We are afflicted in every way, but we are not crushed, uncertain but not in despair. (2 Cor 4:8)

Do we owe God love?

Our belief in God's love requires a response of love. We love God above all others and we love them for love of him. (2093)

And now, Israel, what does the LORD your God require of you, but to fear the LORD your God, to walk in all his ways, to love him, to serve the LORD your God with all your heart and with all your soul. (Dt 10:12)

How do we sin against love?

We sin against love in many ways: by hating God or our neighbor, by envy, sloth, ingratitude, giving scandal, etc. (2094)

You shall not hate your brother in your heart, but you shall reason with your neighbor, lest you bear sin because of him. You shall not take vengeance or bear any grudge against . . . your own people, but you shall love your neighbor as yourself: I am the LORD. (Lev 19:17–18)

What is adoration?

Adoration is the worship we give to God alone as the infinitely holy and Supreme Being. (2096–2097)

Hear, O Israel: The LORD our God is one LORD; and you shall love the LORD your God with all your heart and with all your soul, and with all your might. (Dt 6:4–5)

How do we worship God?

We worship God with public and private prayer, especially the Mass or Eucharistic Celebration, and with acts of faith, hope, and charity. (2098)

What are the main reasons for praying?

The main reasons for praying are to adore God, to thank him, to ask his forgiveness and make up for sin, and to ask his help for ourselves and others. (2098)

Then he told them a parable about the need for them to pray always and not become discouraged. (Lk 18:1)

Is sacrifice a form of prayer?

Sacrifice is a sign of our prayer, adoration, thanksgiving, contrition, or supplication. We unite our sacrifices to the one true and indispensable sacrifice of Jesus on the cross. (2099–2100)

He presented himself as an unblemished offering to God and will purify our consciences from ineffective practices so that we'll be fit to worship the living God. (Heb 9:14)

What is a vow?

A vow is a free and deliberate promise made to God. It is "an act of *devotion* in which the Christian dedicates himself to God or promises him some good work." (2102)

> *You shall be careful to perform what has passed your lips, for you have voluntarily vowed to the LORD your God what you have promised with your mouth.* (Dt 23:23)

What kinds of vows are there?

There are two kinds of vows: public vows which are accepted in the name of the Church by a lawful religious superior, and private vows which an individual makes directly to God. Examples of public vows are those made by a couple in marriage, or by a consecrated religious at profession. A private vow may be to perform a specific religious or charitable act.

What vows do religious make?

Religious make three vows: chastity (not to marry, for the sake of the kingdom), poverty (to give up ownership of material goods), and obedience (to obey their superiors, who hold God's place). These vows are promises to live the evangelical counsels. (2103)

Do we make promises to God?

We do make promises to God, such as the baptismal promises, or the promises made in Marriage or Holy Orders. Some people also make promises to fulfill a certain religious act: a pilgrimage, support of a good work, certain prayers, etc. These are acts made out of love and respect for the goodness of God. (2101)

May we disregard the fulfillment of our vows?

We may not disregard the fulfillment of our vows. To do so would be sinful, more or less grievous, according to the nature of the vow and the intention we had when we made it.

Can we be dispensed from vows and promises?

The Church can and sometimes does dispense from vows and promises for serious reasons. The person seeking a dispensation must apply to the proper religious or ecclesial authority. (2103)

Is religious freedom a right?

Yes, every person has the right to freely express his or her religious convictions in accordance with conscience. No one may restrain or interfere with the exercise of this right, because it is based on the duty of each person to worship God individually and with the community. (2104–2109)

What is idolatry?

Idolatry is giving to a creature (another human, the devil, a created object, money, power, pleasure) the supreme honor due to God alone. (2112–2114)

You cannot serve God and mammon! (Mt 6:24)

What is superstition?

Superstition is failing to render God the honor due him by placing too much trust in external practices or religious objects. (2111)

In what other ways can we fail to honor God?

We would dishonor God if we attributed to creatures powers that belong to God alone, by believing in horoscopes, dreams, crystal gazing, charms, and the like; by consulting spiritualists; by using magic; by satanism, which is invoking the devil. (2115–2117)

> *There shall not be found among you . . . any one who practices divination, a soothsayer, or an augur, or a sorcerer, or a charmer, or a medium, or a wizard, or a necromancer. For whoever does these things is an abomination to the LORD.* (Dt 18:10–12)

What are the main sins of irreligion?

The main sins of irreligion are:

* ❖ *tempting God,* which is testing him by word or deed, setting up a challenge to God's power or loving care; (2119)
* ❖ *sacrilege,* which is the abuse of a person, place, or thing consecrated to God and his service; (2120)
* ❖ *simony,* which is the buying and selling of sacred things. (2121)

Is it simony to give money to have Masses offered?

It is not simony to give money to have Masses offered because the money is not buying the sacrament. It is a courtesy offering used to defray expenses and is not required of the poor. (2122)

> *The worker is deserving of his living.* (Mt 10:10)

Who is an atheist?

An atheist is a person who claims that there is no God or at least lives as though God does not exist. (2123–2126)

Who is an agnostic?

An agnostic is a person who thinks that we cannot know whether God exists or not. (2127)

> *From the creation of the world God's invisible attributes—his eternal power and divine nature—have been accessible to human*

knowledge through what can be perceived, and so they have no excuse. (Rom 1:20)

What is indifferentism?

Indifferentism is the idea that religion is unimportant or the belief that one religion is as good as another. (2128)

What is infidelity?

Infidelity is unfaithfulness or disloyalty, in this case, to God.

How can we help to bring unbelievers to God?

We can help to bring unbelievers to God by prayer, by the witness of our lives, and by being informed Catholics who are willing to share our knowledge of the faith with others.

In venerating relics and sacred images, do we pray to or adore them?

We do not pray to or adore relics and sacred images, but we honor and pray to the persons whom they represent. (2129–2132)

Second Commandment

What is the second commandment of God?

The second commandment of God is:

You shall not take the name of the LORD your God in vain. (Ex 20:7)

What did Jesus say about the second commandment?

Jesus said:

"You have heard that it was said to your ancestors, 'You shall not break your oaths'. . . . But I tell you not to swear at all." (Mt 5:33–34)

What does the second commandment require of us?

The second commandment requires us always to speak reverently of God, to respect his name, and all that is sacred. (2142–2144)

Blessed be the name of the LORD from this time forth and for evermore. (Ps 113:2)

What does the second commandment forbid?

The second commandment forbids improper use of the names of God, Jesus Christ, the Virgin Mary, the angels, and the saints. (2146)

What else does the second commandment require of us?

The second commandment also requires us to be truthful in taking oaths and faithful in fulfilling vows. (2145)

Do not swear, whether by heaven, earth, or some other oath; let your "yes" be "yes" and your "no," "no," lest you come under condemnation. (Jas 5:12)

Why should we speak respectfully of holy persons, places, and things?

Because holy persons, places, and things are consecrated to God, they call for respect and reverence.

May the words of Sacred Scripture ever be used in a bad or disrespectful sense?

The words of Sacred Scripture may never be used in a bad or disrespectful sense. Neither should they be ridiculed, used for jokes nor given any other meaning than what we believe God intended.

What is blasphemy?

Blasphemy is any word, thought, or action that shows contempt for God, the Blessed Virgin, the angels, saints, or religion. (2148)

Whoever curses his God shall bear his sin. (Lev 24:15)

What two conditions are necessary for blasphemy to occur?

Two conditions necessary for blasphemy to occur are: (1) knowledge of God and the sacred; (2) deliberate contempt for the same.

What is cursing?

Cursing is calling down evil on some person, place, or thing.

Is the cursing of animals or inanimate objects sinful?

The cursing of animals or inanimate objects is sinful because of the lack of virtue shown in uncontrolled anger or impatience.

Is cursing another person with moral or physical evil sinful?

To curse another person with moral or physical evil is always sinful according to the degree of intent in wishing the evil.

What is profanity?

Profanity is the irreverent use of the name of God, Jesus Christ, or the saints through impatience, jest, surprise, or habit. (2148–2150)

What is an oath?

An oath is a declaration before God that what we say is true. (2149)

Men swear in the name of someone greater than themselves, and the oath serves as a guarantee to put an end to any dispute. (Heb 6:16)

Is it lawful to take an oath?

It is lawful to take an oath because it is a guarantee of the truth. This is expected in a court of law. (2153–2154)

You shall fear the LORD your God; you shall serve him, and swear by his name. (Dt 6:13)

What conditions make an oath lawful?

The conditions which make an oath lawful are sufficient reason for taking an oath, conviction that we speak the truth, and having a good intention, not a sinful one, for taking the oath.

And if you swear, "As the LORD lives," in truth, in justice, and in uprightness, then nations shall bless themselves in him, and in him shall they glory. (Jer 4:2)

When may an oath be taken?

An oath may be taken when it concerns the glory of God, the good of our neighbor or our own personal good.

Is an unlawful oath or vow binding?

An unlawful oath or vow is not binding. Such oaths or vows are not to be taken, and to fulfill them is sinful because we are misusing God's name to support a lie. (2151)

What is perjury?

Perjury is calling upon God to bear witness to a lie. Perjury is also committed when, while under oath, one confirms with certainty something that is unknown or doubtful. (2152)

And you shall not swear by my name falsely, and so profane the name of your God: I am the LORD. (Lev 19:12)

Is a Christian's name also holy?

Yes, the name "Christian" is holy because it refers to Jesus, the Holy One of God. The individual Christian's name is also holy because it was received in the name of the Trinity in Baptism. (2156–2159)

> *Behold I saw the Lamb standing on Mount Zion, and with him was a crowd one hundred and forty-four thousand strong, each of whom had the Lamb's name and the name of the Lamb's Father written on their foreheads.* (Rev 14:1)

Third Commandment

What is the third commandment of God?

The third commandment of God is:

> *Remember the sabbath day, to keep it holy.. for in six days the Lord made heaven and earth, the sea, and all that is in them, and rested the seventh day: therefore the* LORD *blessed the sabbath day and hallowed it.* (Ex 20:8, 11)

What did Jesus say about the third commandment?

Jesus said:

> *"The sabbath was made for man, not man for the sabbath; thus the Son of Man is Lord even of the Sabbath."* (Mk 2:27–28)

What does the third commandment require of us?

The third commandment requires us to celebrate the holiness of the Lord's Day by observing it as a day of rest. As the *Catechism of the Catholic Church* says: "The sabbath is for the Lord, holy and set apart for the praise of God, his work of creation, and his saving actions on behalf of Israel." (2171)

(What is said in this section about Sundays applies also to holy days of obligation.)

Six days shall work be done, but the seventh day is a sabbath of solemn rest, holy to the Lord. (Ex 31:15)

What does the third commandment tell us to avoid?

We should abstain from work or business that would impede worship of God, the joy proper to the Lord's Day, or the proper relaxation of mind and body. (2185)

And on the seventh day he rested, and was refreshed. (Ex 31:17)

Is it necessary to worship God?

Yes, the worship of God is a duty inscribed on the human heart. In gratitude for God's goodness and providence we owe public, communal worship. The Sunday rest is the natural opportunity because it is the day we dedicate to God. (2176)

Do not neglect your assemblies, as some are in the habit of doing; encourage one another. (Heb 10:25)

Why do Christians celebrate Sunday and not Saturday?

Christians celebrate on Sunday because it is the day of Christ's resurrection, which began a new creation, a new covenant with us. (2174–2175)

Now after the sabbath, as it began to dawn on the first day of the week, Mary Magdalen and the other Mary came to see the sepulchre. (Mt 28:1)

Are Catholics obliged to participate in Mass on Sunday?

Church law obliges Catholics to participate in Mass on Sundays and holy days (or on the previous evening). To deliberately miss Mass is a grave sin. To be excused from attendance requires a weighty reason such as serious illness or grave inconvenience, or being dispensed by one's pastor. (2180–2181)

Why is it spiritually unwise to easily exempt ourselves from Sunday Mass?

It is spiritually unwise to easily exempt ourselves from Sunday Mass because the graces that we need to live fervent Catholic lives come to us through the Mass. (2182)

Who are exempt from participating in Sunday or holy day Mass?

Some of those exempted from participating in Sunday or holy day Mass are the sick and those who must care for them, those who live a great distance from a Catholic Church, those who have urgent work (policemen, firemen, medical personnel on duty, etc.), and those hampered by temporary difficulties such as weather. Anyone may freely consult a priest about his or her particular situation, and is encouraged to do so. (2181)

What is the Mass?

The Mass is the sacrifice of Calvary made present on our altars so that we may share in the benefits of the redemption; it is a memorial of the death and resurrection of Christ and a sacred banquet in which Christ is received. (See section on the Eucharist, pages 96-116.)

What is the best way of participating in the Mass?

The best way of participating in the Mass is to offer it to God in union with the priest and the entire faith community, uniting oneself interiorly and exteriorly with Christ the Victim, and by receiving him in Holy Communion.

How is the unity of God's people expressed in the Mass?

The unity of God's people is expressed by the actions of the faithful who pray, sing, and act together in the Mass. Most of all, it is expressed in receiving the Holy Eucharist, which is the center of unity.

Can we not worship God in our own hearts instead of participating at Mass?

Interior worship is not enough, for God created us as social beings. Our unity in the Church calls us to worship with the community.

What activities are especially suited to make Sunday a holy day?

Reading a good book, doing works of charity, cultivating our cultural interests, and enjoying wholesome recreation are some activities suited for Sundays. (2186)

Fourth Commandment

What is the fourth commandment of God?

The fourth commandment of God is:

Honor your father and your mother, that your days may be long in the land which the LORD your God gives you. (Ex 20:12)

What does Jesus teach about the fourth commandment?

Jesus lived this commandment:

Then he went down with them and went to Nazareth, and he was subject to them. (Lk 2:51)

What does the fourth commandment require of us?

The fourth commandment obliges us to love our parents, respect and obey them in all that is not contrary to God's law, and help them in their needs. It presupposes that parents and all others in authority will fulfill their duties justly. (2197)

What does the fourth commandment forbid?

The fourth commandment forbids all disrespect, unkindness, stubbornness, spitefulness, hatred, and disobedience toward our parents and lawful authorities.

What is the source of parental authority?

God himself is the source of parental authority, so children have a strict moral obligation to obey and care for their parents. (2214)

Remember, her [your mother], my son, because she faced many dangers for you while you were in her womb. (Tob 4:4)

How do children show love and respect for their parents?

Children show love and respect for their parents when they give them gratitude, love and care, readily accept corrections, seek advice in important decisions, patiently bear with their parents' faults, and pray for them. (2215–2216)

With all your heart honor your father, and do not forget the birth pangs of your mother. Remember that it was of your parents you were born: how can you repay what they have given you? (Sir 7:27–28)

Are we obliged to respect and obey others besides our parents?

Besides our parents, the fourth commandment obliges us to respect and obey our teachers and lawful superiors, civil and ecclesiastical, when they discharge their official duties in conformity with the law of God. We also owe particular gratitude to grandparents, godparents, family members, pastors, and friends. (2199–2220)

Every person should be subject to the governing authorities. For all authority comes from God and the existing authorities have been appointed by God. Therefore, whoever resists authority resists God's order, and those who resist will bring judgment upon themselves. (Rom 13:1–2)

Are children obliged to obey their parents about their choice of a state in life?

Children should ordinarily ask their parents' advice about their choice of a state in life, but they are free to make their own decisions. Parents must not force their children in this matter, but encourage them to welcome the Lord's call, whether to marriage, the single life, priesthood, or religious life. (2230, 2232–2233)

> *Whoever loves his father or mother more than me is not worthy of me, and whoever loves his son or daughter more than me is not worthy of me.* (Mt 10:37)

What duties do adults owe their parents?

Adults continue to owe love and respect to their parents. If possible, grown children must help their needy parents materially and morally, especially in old age, illness, or other difficulties. (2218)

> *The glory of one's father is one's own glory, and it is a disgrace for children not to respect their mother.* (Sir 3:11)

What are the duties of parents toward their children?

Parents must love their children, have them baptized, provide for their emotional, spiritual, and physical needs, instruct them and give them a Christian education, train them by word and example in the practice of Christian virtue, and counsel and guide them in forming a correct moral conscience. (2221–2229)

> *Fathers, do not cause your children to resent you; instead, raise them by instructing and admonishing them as the Lord would.* (Eph 6:4)

How can parents foster family unity?

Parents can foster family unity by family prayer and by loving each other and their children. (2226)

Are we obliged to obey civil laws when they are contrary to God's law?

If the civil law obliges citizens to violate the law of God, they must refuse to obey. (2242)

We have to obey God rather than men. (Acts 5:29)

What are the duties of citizens toward their country?

The principal duties of citizens toward their country are to respect civil authority and obey just laws, that is, conscientiously fulfill all civil duties. (2239)

Then render to Caesar the things that are Caesar's and to God the things that are God's. (Lk 20:25)

What are the principal civil duties?

The principal civil duties are to pay taxes; to defend one's country, even at the cost of one's life; to fulfill one's duty of voting; to work for and support laws that protect Christian morals and the common good. Insofar as possible, Catholics must vote for people whose beliefs and programs are truly beneficial to everyone. (2240)

Pay everyone what you owe—taxes to the tax collectors, customs duties to the customs officials; respect those to whom it is due, honor those to whom honor is due. (Rom 13:7)

Fifth Commandment

What is the fifth commandment of God?

The fifth commandment of God is:

You shall not kill. (Ex 20:13)

What did Jesus say about the fifth commandment?

Jesus said:

You have heard that it was said to the ancients, "You shall not murder," and that whoever does commit murder shall be liable to judgment. But I say to you, anyone who is angry with his brother shall be liable to judgment, and whoever says to his brother, "Raqa!" shall be liable to the Sanhedrin, and whoever says, "You fool!" shall be liable to the fire of Gehenna. (Mt 5:21–22)

What does the fifth commandment require of us?

The fifth commandment requires us to respect the sacredness of human life in all its stages, and to take proper care of our own life and the lives of others. (2258)

In his hand is the life of every living thing and the breath of every human being. (Job 12:10 NRSV)

Are we to respect all people?

All people deserve respect because they are created in the image and likeness of God, have been redeemed by Christ, and are destined for eternal life. Every type of prejudice is to be overcome and rooted out as contrary to God's intent and to human dignity.

This is the commandment just as you heard from the beginning— that you should walk in love. (2 Jn 6)

What are some of the chief crimes committed against human life and dignity?

Some of the chief crimes committed against human life and dignity are any type of murder, including abortion, euthanasia or "mercy-killing"; culpable suicide; direct sterilization; mutilation of the human body without a serious reason; torture and brainwashing; fomenting indecent living and working conditions; forced imprisonment of innocent people; unjust deportation from one's own country; slavery; and the selling of men, women, and children (human trafficking).

What is murder?

Murder is direct and intentional killing of a human being. Murderers and those who cooperate with them commit grave sin, as does anyone who indirectly contributes to another person's death. (2268–2269)

> But as for . . . murderers . . . their portion lies in the flaming lake of fire and sulfur, that is, the second death. (Rev 21:8)

Does the commandment "you shall not kill" apply to all innocent human life?

This commandment applies to all innocent human life, including that of the unborn child, who has the same right to life as any other person. Abortion at any time after the child is conceived deprives the unborn of this basic right, and therefore is murder. (2270)

> Before I formed you in the womb I knew you, and before you were born I consecrated you. (Jer 1:5)

Do those who cooperate in an abortion share the guilt?

Those who formally cooperate in an abortion (who participate in the act itself in some way and approve it, such as the abortionist, abortion clinic personnel, etc.) commit a grave offense and are, by the act, excommunicated from the Church. (2272)

> There are . . . things which the LORD hates . . . which are an abomination to him: haughty eyes, a lying tongue, and hands that shed innocent blood. . . . (Prov 6:16–17)

Do parents have legal rights over an unborn child?

Parents have parental rights over the unborn child, but these are all positive and supportive, such as to name, educate, and protect the child. Neither parents, doctors, nor the State can deprive the unborn of their inalienable right to life. This right is inherent in human nature, originating in the parent's creative act. No one else has any right over another's life or bodily integrity; neither can the State presume to give such rights by law. (2273)

Is abortion allowable for rape, incest, or to save a mother's life?

In the case of rape or incest, certain immediate steps can be taken to prevent conception. If these efforts fail, however, abortion can never be the next step. The new life is innocent and independent of the sinful act. Neither can an abortion be performed to save the mother's life. Sometimes a medical procedure used in treating the mother may indirectly cause an abortion, but nothing may be done to induce a direct abortion.

What is to be said of experiments on the human embryo?

The utmost care and respect is due to the human embryo, which must be treated as a person from its conception. The human embryo must not be produced for experimentation nor disposed of as biological waste. Genetic manipulation and selection are to be condemned. Only what is truly therapeutic can be considered licit. (2274–2275)

Is euthanasia or "mercy-killing" against the fifth commandment?

Euthanasia or "mercy-killing" is always a grave sin because no human person has the right to take his or her own life or that of another. God alone is the Lord and Master of life. The sin committed is either suicide or murder. We must be attentive to the rightful care of the elderly and infirm, and guard against neglect or attempts to shorten their lives. (2276)

Is suicide contrary to God's law?

Suicide is contrary to the law of God who is the sovereign master of life. We are only stewards of our life, charged with the duty to preserve it. (2280–2281)

Can any circumstances mitigate the guilt of suicide?

The guilt of suicide can be mitigated by severe psychological illness, anxiety, fear, suffering, or torture. The Church encourages us to pray for those who commit suicide, believing that God provides an opportunity for repentance before they die. (2282–2283)

Is scandal sinful?

To give scandal or serious bad example by leading another to sin by word, action, or omission, or by lessening another's respect for God and religion, can be sinful. (2284)

For scandal not to come is impossible, but woe to the one through whom it comes! It would be better for him to have a millstone placed around his neck and be thrown into the sea. (Lk 17:1–2)

What are some sources of scandal?

Some sources of scandal or bad example are immoral behavior by an authority figure, improper language or hate-filled speech, immoral literature or media programs, immodest styles, dishonest business practices, etc. (2285–2286)

How are we to take care of our physical health?

We should use ordinary means (food, sleep, shelter, medical attention) to preserve our life. We must avoid an exaggerated "cult of the body," that is, excessive concern about physical appearance and bodily well-being. Dangerous sports, intemperance in food and drink, smoking and reckless driving, etc., are to be avoided because they endanger our life and health or that of others. (2288)

Why must we treat our body as a sacred thing?

We must treat our body as a sacred thing because it truly is, since God lives within us by grace. St. Paul says:

> Or do you not know that your bodies are temples of the Holy Spirit. (1 Cor 6:19)

Is it ever permissible to knowingly shorten one's life?

It is sinful to directly intend to shorten one's life, such as by choosing to work under dangerous conditions in the hope of shortening one's own life. But a person may risk his life or health for a serious motive, for example, to save the life of another person.

> Greater love than this no man has—to lay down his life for his friends. (Jn 15:13)

Can we ever refuse medical treatment?

Yes, we can refuse medical treatment that is burdensome, extraordinary, or disproportionate to the expected results. The decision belongs to the patient, or if the patient is no longer competent, to a trusted person who knows the patient's wishes or best interests in this regard. (2278)

Is it permissible for the dying to take painkillers, even if such drugs might shorten their life?

The dying may take painkillers to alleviate the intense sufferings that often accompany the process of dying. They must not be taken with the intention of hastening death, but to make the person more comfortable in the face of inevitable death. (2279)

Is drug abuse sinful?

Drug abuse is sinful because it can seriously injure our mental and/or physical well-being. Drugs also make it easy for us to do wrong to ourselves or to others. (2291)

Is mutilation of the human body ever permitted?

Mutilation of the human body—for example, removing an arm, leg, etc.—may be permitted if there is no other way to preserve the health or save the life of a person. Other forms of mutilation such as tattoos or piercings should be carefully considered because of the possible risks to health. Also, one would not want to desecrate the body with evil signs or images. (2297)

Should medical research be encouraged?

Medical and scientific research should be encouraged because of its potential for alleviating human suffering. All research and experimentation must be done in conformity with human dignity and moral law. (2295)

What does the Church teach about organ donation?

Organ donation is morally acceptable and can be meritorious because of the benefit to the recipient. Consent, however, must be given by the donor or a legitimate spokesperson. The donor may not be mutilated nor may death be caused by the donation. (2296)

What other crimes are there against bodily integrity?

Terrorism, torture, kidnapping, hostage taking, issuing false threats, and acts of violence, such as mutilation, are gravely sinful. (2297–2298)

What is owed to the dying?

We owe care and respect to the dying and the support of our prayers. The dying should be given the opportunity to receive the sacraments of the sick. (2299)

What is proper treatment of the dead?

The dead must be treated with the respect due to them as God's children now awaiting resurrection. The burial should be conducted with dignity. Cremation is also permitted, provided it is not a denial of bodily resurrection. (2300–2301)

Is it ever permitted to take the life of another person?

Although it is never permissible to take an innocent life, in some circumstances it may be lawful to take the life of another person. For example, an act of self-defense may result in unintentional killing. Legitimate defense may include:

❖ protecting one's own life and possessions and those of one's neighbor from an unjust attacker, provided no other means of protection is effective;

- ❖ fighting a just war;
- ❖ executing just punishment for a crime, though many Catholic thinkers hold that capital punishment is no longer justifiable in our society. (2263–2266)

What must we consider concerning capital punishment?

Although imposing capital punishment has long been recognized as a legitimate right of civil authorities for punishing grave crimes, we must consider whether or not the accused will profit by another form of punishment such as life imprisonment in order to reflect and repent; that the accused may actually be innocent; that our motivations may be spiritually injurious to ourselves or others, such as revenge or hatred; that the example of imposing death may prove counterproductive by lessening the general respect for life rather than lowering the crime rate. The *Catechism of the Catholic Church* states: "Today . . . the cases in which the execution of the offender is an absolute necessity 'are very rare, if not practically non-existent.'" (2266–2267)

Does this commandment forbid war?

The fifth commandment forbids intentional killing; therefore, war can never be pursued without extremely grave reasons, for example, acts of terrorism. Everyone has the duty to avoid war, if at all possible. (2307–2308)

When is a war just?

For a war to be just, it must be called for by the head of the government; those who are undertaking war should have a rightful intention; there must be a just cause; other means of settlement must have been tried and failed; the evils of conflict must not outweigh the good results to be expected from waging war; and there must be "serious prospects of success."

Applying those principles is very difficult today, especially because of the nature of modern weapons. (2309)

How can Christians promote true peace?

Christians can promote true peace by rooting out all causes of discord (injustice, distrust, pride, envy, and other selfish passions) in their own lives; they can also offer financial, professional, and moral support to national and international institutes whose aim is to aid developing nations and work for cooperation among nations. (2304–2306)

How should military personnel act in a war?

War does not excuse combatants from the moral law. Military personnel must never act in blind obedience when ordered to commit atrocities such as genocide, which is a grave sin. Civilians, prisoners, and the wounded must be treated humanely. Total destruction of cities is condemned. (2313–2314)

Is it immoral to accumulate arms?

The over-accumulation of arms is immoral because it increases the risk of conflict, and the expense impoverishes the peoples involved. Further, the production and sale of armaments often promotes violence and conflict among developing nations. (2315–2316)

> He shall judge between the nations, and shall decide for many peoples; and they shall beat their swords into plowshares, and their spears into pruning hooks; nations shall not lift up sword against nation, neither shall they learn war any more. (Is 2:4)

Is the obligation of bearing arms in the service of one's country binding upon all?

The obligation to serve one's country allows for those who, for reasons of conscience, refuse to bear arms, provided that they agree to serve the community in some other way. (2311)

How important is our spiritual well-being?

Our spiritual well-being is even more important than our physical well-being because life is a gift from God, and we are not destined for this life alone but for eternal life.

What else is opposed to the fifth commandment?

Quarreling, fighting, anger, hatred, revenge, drunkenness, and taking or dealing in drugs or other harmful substances are opposed to this commandment. (2302–2303)

What did Christ teach us about love and forgiveness?

Christ taught us to pray in the Our Father: "Forgive us our trespasses, as we forgive those who trespass against us."

He has given us the supreme example: From the cross he prayed for all those responsible for his death: "Father, forgive them, for they do not know what they are doing" (Lk 23:34). He also said: "Love your enemies, and pray for those who persecute you." (Mt 5:44) (2305)

Why are anger and hatred contrary to the fifth commandment?

Anger and hatred intend harm or evil to another person, which is directly contrary to the peace this commandment requires. The sin of anger is not to be confused with the emotion that comes up spontaneously. (2302–2303)

> *"You have heard that it was said 'Love your neighbor and hate your enemy.' But I say to you, love your enemies, and pray for those who persecute you. . . ."* (Mt 5:43–44)

Sixth Commandment

What is the sixth commandment of God?

The sixth commandment of God is:

You shall not commit adultery. (Ex 20:14)

What did Jesus say about the sixth commandment?

Jesus said:

"You have heard that it was said, 'You shall not commit adultery!' But I say to you that anyone who looks at a woman with lust for her has already committed adultery with her in his heart." (Mt 5:27–28)

What does the sixth commandment require of us?

The sixth commandment requires us to be chaste and modest in behavior both when alone and with others.

What is chastity?

Chastity is that virtue by which we properly regulate our use of sexuality according to our state in life. Chastity consists in the inner harmony of one's body and soul, as well as "the successful integration of sexuality within the person." (2337–2345, 2348–2350)

For all of you who were baptized into Christ have clothed yourselves with Christ. (Gal 3:27)

How important is sexuality?

Our human sexuality is an extraordinary gift of God. It affects every other aspect of who we are. Through our maleness or femaleness we express our vocation to love and to community. It is important to understand and accept our sexual identity in order to assume our proper role in marriage, the family, and society. (2331–2332)

> *So God created man in his own image, in the image of God he created him; male and female he created them. And God blessed them, and God said to them, "Be fruitful and multiply, and fill the earth and subdue it." (Gen 1:27–28)*

How should the engaged observe chastity?

Those engaged to be married must continue to live the chastity of continence proper to all those not married. By saving the special expressions of marital love for after the wedding, they will strengthen their mutual love, fidelity, and commitment. (2350)

Is it sinful to move in with another person and engage in sexual acts outside of marriage?

Yes, it is sinful to engage in marital acts outside of marriage. Unfortunately, many couples have accepted this mode of cohabitation as a normal expression of love. However, it is a sin against the sixth commandment.

What are the main sins against chastity?

The sixth commandment forbids sexual acts outside of marriage. Among the sins against chastity are:

- ❖ *lust*—the inordinate desire and pursuit of sexual pleasure for its own sake, which is contrary to the unitive and procreative ends of the sexual acts; (2351)
- ❖ *masturbation*—the stimulation of one's genital organs to induce pleasure, which is contrary to the self-gift and openness to life essential to such acts; (2352)
- ❖ *fornication*—sexual intercourse between an unmarried man and an unmarried woman, which is contrary to the

dignity of those involved and to marriage itself. It may also give scandal; (2353)

❖ *pornography*—the display of sexual acts for profit, which harms the dignity of the person and the marital act, and causes grave scandal. Pornography often involves the abuse and exploitation of children and teenagers, and those who purchase it participate in this grave evil; (2354)

❖ *prostitution*—the use of one's body for the sexual pleasure of a client, which reduces personal dignity to the level of a commodity. Poor economic and social conditions may pressure persons into prostitution, and those who pay for sex bear a grave responsibility for perpetuating these evils; (2355)

❖ *rape*—sexual force used against an unwilling victim, which violates the privacy and integrity of another, often causing lasting injury to the victim. (2356)

Don't you know that your bodies are temples of the Holy Spirit within you, who comes to you from God, and that you do not belong to yourselves? You were bought for a price, so glorify God in your bodies! (1 Cor 6:19–20)

Why are homosexual acts contrary to the sixth commandment?

Homosexual acts, which are sexual acts of men or women with persons of the same sex, are contrary to this commandment, first, because the two persons are not married; and second, because these unions are not open to the gift of life nor do they build on the complementarity of the sexes, concepts essential to sexual activity. (2357)

Their women exchanged natural relations for unnatural, and the men likewise gave up natural relations with women and were consumed with passion for one another. . . . (Rom 1:26–27)

Why does the Church forbid same-sex marriage?

The Church cannot condone or permit marriage between persons of the same sex because of the nature of marriage, which is ordered to the procreation of children. The marriage act itself is impossible in such a union. Marriage between a man and a woman was created by God "from the begininning."

"Haven't you read that from the beginning the Creator made them male and female? And he [Jesus] said, 'For this reason a man shall leave father and mother and be united with his wife, and the two shall become one flesh.'" (Mt 19:4-5)

How should homosexual persons be treated?

While homosexual acts must be considered gravely sinful, a homosexual person must be treated with the same love and respect we owe to everyone in Christ's name. (2357–2359)

What are the two purposes of marriage?

The two purposes of marriage are the love and fidelity of the couple, which bring them joy and fulfillment in their relationship, and fecundity, which is the transmission and nurturing of new life. (See also the section on the sacrament of Matrimony, pages 139–149.) (2360–2367)

You made Adam, and for him you made his wife Eve as a helper and support. (Tob 8:6)

What is the Church's teaching on contraception?

The Church teaches that all forms of contraception such as pills, drugs, or mechanical devices are sinful because these are against the natural purpose of married love, the transmission or giving of life. If just reasons warrant the limitation of births, Catholics may practice natural family planning (NFP). Couples may consult a priest or Catholic natural family planning groups. (2368–2370)

What is the difference between contraception and NFP, if the purpose of limiting births is the same?

If a person needs money, it makes a great moral difference to obtain it by working or by stealing, for these are two different types of moral acts. Similarly, though the intention to limit births may be the same, contraception and NFP are two different kinds of moral acts. In contraception, a naturally fertile act is deliberately rendered sterile by some outside means. This breaks the connection between the life-giving and love-giving aspects of marital intercourse, in such a way that the language of the body is saying one thing, but the contraceptive element is saying another. In NFP, couples do not break this connection but simply abstain during fertile times.

May the State make laws regulating births?

No, the State may not make laws regulating births; neither may it coerce couples into limiting the size of their families. The State may make observations concerning its population, but may not impose its will. (2372)

What does the Church teach concerning sterilization?

If direct sterilization, to take away a person's power to have children, is performed for one's own satisfaction or economic or social needs, such actions are grievously wrong. If indirect sterilization is necessary for serious health reasons, no sin is involved since the intent is not to make procreation impossible, and the sterilization comes about as an undesired side effect. (2297, 2399)

What may an infertile couple do about having a child?

Couples who find that they are infertile may engage medical help that respects their marital relationship and the moral law, such as NaProTECHNOLOGY. They must be aware that techniques such as sperm or ovum donation, surrogate motherhood, and artificial insemination or fertilization are gravely sinful because they separate sex and procreation. The dignity and intimacy of the act has been violated, and in some cases the child is deprived of natural family bonds. Rather than resort to such practices, the couple should be encouraged to adopt a child or to dedicate themselves to the service of other people. (2373–2379)

Why is adultery forbidden?

Adultery is a grave injustice to one's spouse. It violates the marital covenant, undermines trust, and harms the children's welfare. (2380–2381)

For God called us to holiness, not to impurity. (1 Thes 4:7)

What is divorce?

Divorce is a serious offense against the natural law because it is an attempt to break the permanent covenant pledged by the husband and wife to be faithful until death. It disregards the sacramental nature of marriage, inflicts suffering upon the deserted spouse and the children, and disrupts society. (2382, 2384–2386)

Whoever divorces his wife and marries another, commits adultery against her; and if she divorces her husband and marries another, she commits adultery. (Mk 10:11–12)

Is divorce ever permitted?

When there is no hope of reconciliation, civil divorce may be allowed as a means of protecting oneself legally and of caring for the children. However, one is not free to remarry. (2383)

The wife should not separate from her husband (but if she does, let her remain single or else be reconciled to her husband)—and that the husband should not divorce his wife. (1 Cor 7:10–11)

Are there other offenses against marriage?

These are other offenses against marriage:

* ❖ *polygamy*—having two or more spouses simultaneously. This offends the original plan of God who made marriage an exclusive relationship; (2387)
* ❖ *incest or child abuse*—having sexual relations with close relatives or with children or adolescents. These grave violations of the moral integrity of the victim cause serious emotional and/or psychological damage; (2388–2389)
* ❖ *"free union"*—exercising marital rights with a partner without any commitments. Such situations breed distrust, infidelity, and irresponsibility, and weaken the moral fiber of society; (2390)
* ❖ *"trial marriage"*—living together as if married while having only a future intention of marriage. This lack of a real commitment undermines the true nature of love and marriage, which requires a total gift. (2391)

Can we not act in sexual matters by our own conscience?

We must certainly judge all our actions by our conscience, but first of all our conscience must be educated according to objective moral truth, that is, by the moral law our Creator gave us. This requires study of the Scriptures and Church teachings and sincere prayer.

> *Whoever keeps my commandments and obeys them—he it is who loves me, while whoever loves me is loved by my Father, and I will love him and reveal myself to him.* (Jn 14:21)

How do we know the Church is right in its judgment on sexual matters?

We know the Church judges rightly on sexual matters because it has a divine mandate from Christ to guard and interpret his moral teachings, and the Holy Spirit aids the Church in this. We also know that Christian moral law is based on natural law, which is the law written in our hearts. (1954–1960)

Whoever hears you, hears me, and whoever rejects you, rejects me. And whoever rejects me, rejects the one who sent me. (Lk 10:16)

Seventh Commandment

What is the seventh commandment of God?

The seventh commandment of God is:

You shall not steal. (Ex 20:15)

What did Jesus say about the seventh commandment?

Jesus warned us to guard against the temptation to steal:

For from the heart come wicked thoughts, murder, adultery, fornication, theft, false witness, and blasphemy. (Mt 15:19)

What does the seventh commandment require of us?

This commandment requires us to be just, charitable, and honest with respect to this world's goods—our own and those of others, and those common to the human family. (2401)

What does the seventh commandment forbid?

The seventh commandment forbids stealing and robbery, the unjust acquisition of goods, reckless destruction of what belongs to others, and disregard for the goods of the earth.

Stealing can be mortally sinful if the thing stolen is of considerable value (otherwise it is a venial sin). Stealing something of small value can be mortally sinful if the owner is poor, and thus suffers great injury.

If you want to enter into life, keep the commandments. . . . "You shall not steal. . . ." (Mt 19:17–18)

Are we bound to return stolen goods?

We are bound to return stolen goods or their value in money to the owner, or, if the owner is dead, to his or her family. If neither the owner nor the family can be discovered, the goods or their value are to be given to the poor or to charitable causes. (2412)

But Zacchaeus stood up and said to the Lord, "Look, Lord, I am giving half of my possessions to the poor, and if I have cheated anyone of anything I am paying back four fold." (Lk 19:8)

Could taking others' property ever be justified?

Taking others' property could be justified only if one is in urgent need of basic necessities, such as food and clothing, and there is no other means of obtaining them. (2408)

What are some more subtle forms of stealing?

Some more subtle forms of stealing are cheating or deceiving the consumer about something being sold, such as hiding a defect in that object; doing poor work or negligent repairs; performing unnecessary repairs; charging a price that deserves a better job; in politics, acquiring money or positions by dishonest means; making false insurance claims; borrowing without returning; tax evasion; forgery; property damage or defacement; waste, etc. (2409)

What virtues serve this commandment?

This commandment will be easier to live if we practice:
* ❖ *temperance*—moderation in acquiring goods;
* ❖ *justice*—respect for the things belonging to another;

❖   *solidarity*—taking the part of the poor, underprivileged or marginalized. (2407)

For you know the grace of our Lord Jesus Christ; although he was rich he became poor for your sake so that you might become rich through his poverty. (2 Cor 8:9)

Do people have a right to private ownership?

Yes, people have a right to private ownership. This right, bestowed by the Creator, provides people with the means for their livelihood, growth, and progress. (2402)

Does the right of private ownership justify the overabundance of some and the extreme poverty of others?

The principle of private ownership does not justify such inequity. No one is justified in keeping for one's exclusive use what is not needed when others lack necessities. The earth belongs to the whole human race. Its division among nations and individuals insures that the rights of everyone will be cared for and protected. (2403–2406)

What is a bribe?

A bribe is offering money or other valuable objects with the intention to corrupt or buy a favor.

You shall not pervert justice; you shall not show partiality; and you shall not take a bribe, for a bribe blinds the eyes of the wise and subverts the cause of the righteous. (Dt 16:19)

What does the Church teach about social justice?

The Church's teaching on social justice rests on the Gospel mandate "you shall love your neighbor as yourself" (Mt 22:39). It directs us to live together while being respectful of the dignity of each individual and concerned for their needs, which include food, clothing, shelter, medical assistance, education, protection, and just recompense for labor.

The Spirit of the Lord is upon me, because he has anointed me to bring the good news to the poor. (Lk 4:18)

What are the basic concerns of Catholic social teaching?

In their document, *Sharing Catholic Social Teaching* (4-6), the United States Conference of Catholic Bishops summarizes this teaching in seven themes: "(1) life and dignity of the human person; (2) call to family, community, and participation; (3) rights and respsonsibilities; (4) the option for the poor and vulnerable; (5) the dignity of work and the rights of workers; (6) solidarity; and (7) care for God's creation."

For I was hungry and you gave me to eat, I was thirsty and you gave me to drink, I was a stranger and you took me in, naked and you clothed me, I was sick and you cared for me, I was in prison and you came to me. (Mt 25:35-36)

What does the Church teach about immigration?

Basing herself on God's revelation and natural law, the Church teaches that all have the right to migrate in order to sustain themselves and their families. Nations, however, also have the right to regulate their own borders and thus limit immigration, but nations must exercise this right with justice and mercy.

Are there other values that regulate immigration?

Yes, immigration regulation must make every attempt to keep families together, especially when young children are involved. Needs of immigrants must be met in accord with Christian compassion, that is, the basic need for food, clothing, shelter, medical care, education, and justice. It is immoral to imprison or treat as criminals those who simply seek a better life.

Those who are generous are blessed, for they share their bread with the poor. (Prov 22:9 NRSV)

What value does work have?

Work is a part of human dignity. It gives us a share in God's creative plan, allows us to participate in Christ's redemptive work, and helps us reach holiness by elevating whatever we do to a work of praise. (2426–2428)

What duties do employees have toward their employers?

Workers are to produce good work, use their working hours productively, serve their employers faithfully and honestly, and guard against injury to the property and good name of their employer.

What duties do employers have toward their workers?

Employers must treat their workers fairly and justly, pay them just wages, and provide proper and dignified working conditions with reasonable safety on the job.

When are workers permitted to strike?

Workers are permitted to strike when their rights are violated, lawful contracts ignored, or other serious difficulties arise. The strike, however, can be used only after all other means to solve the difficulties have been exhausted. Moreover, a strike must be conducted in a fair and peaceful manner, avoiding all forms of violence. (2435)

How might workers be exploited?

Persons or their work can be exploited by enslavement, in which individuals are treated like merchandise. This enslavement can be more subtle, as when people are forced to work long hours in poor conditions for meager wages and no benefits because they are illegal aliens, mentally incompetent, or socially marginalized. This is a sin against the dignity of the person and against basic justice. (2414)

> *Perhaps the reason he was taken from you for a time was so you could have him back forever, no longer as a slave but as more than a slave—as a beloved brother.* (Philem 15–16)

What is commutative justice?

Commutative or strict justice is the honor and respect with which we deal with one another. It regulates our contracts, sales, debts, and exchanges. If justice is not strictly practiced on this level, it will not succeed on any other level. (2411)

> *You shall not have in your house two kinds of measures, a large and a small. A full and just weight you shall have, a full and just measure you shall have.* (Dt 25:14–15)

What is legal justice?

Legal justice refers to the conduct of each individual toward society: caring for public property, paying a fair share in taxes, doing community service, carrying out civic responsibilities, defending one's country, etc.

> *For the Lord's sake be subject to every human institution. . . . Live as free men, but without using your freedom as an excuse for evil; instead, conduct yourselves as servants of God. Respect everyone, love the brotherhood, fear God, and honor the emperor.* (1 Pt 2:13, 16–17)

What is distributive justice?

Distributive justice concerns the way a society deals equitably with its individual members.

> *Hear this, you who trample upon the needy, and bring the poor of the land to an end. . . .* (Amos 8:4)

Is one obliged to make up for damage done?

One is obliged to make up for damage unjustly done to the property of others, as far as one is able.

Why does the Church speak about economics?

The Church has the duty to speak about economic and social affairs when the dignity of human persons, their rights, and salvation are at stake. The Church does not side with any government nor prefer any system of governing. Its concern is that we work for a just society and not be impeded in our pursuit of the sovereign Good. (2419–2425)

What is gambling?

Gambling is the staking of money or valuables on a future event or on a game of chance, the result of which is unknown to the participants.

Is it wrong to gamble?

Gambling in itself can be an amusement, and it is not against Catholic moral standards if played fairly, honestly, and with moderation. However, gambling can become a sin, even a mortal sin, if it leads one to excesses such as dishonesty and great loss of money, risking the needs of the family and even of society. (2413)

How should we treat the rest of creation?

All of creation—the animals, plants, minerals—must be respected as part of God's handiwork. We can use them according to need, but must never treat them recklessly or cruelly. We are stewards over creation, to cultivate and sustain it as an inheritance for future generations. Support of ecological initiatives is to be encouraged. (2415–2417)

*And God blessed them, and God said to them, "Be fruitful and mul-
tiply, and fill the earth and subdue it, and have dominion over the
fish of the sea and over the birds of the air and over every living
thing that moves upon the earth." (Gen 1:28)*

Eighth Commandment

What is the eighth commandment of God?

The eighth commandment of God is:

You shall not bear false witness against your neighbor. (Ex 20:16)

What did Jesus say about the eighth commandment?

Jesus said:

*"Again, you have heard that it was said to your ancestors, 'You shall
not break your oaths!' and 'You shall fulfill your oaths to the Lord!'
But I tell you not to swear at all, neither by heaven, because it is the
throne of God, nor by the earth, because it is the footstool for his feet,
nor by Jerusalem, because it is the city of the Great King, nor shall
you swear by your head, because you are not able to make one hair
white or black. Let your 'yes,' be 'yes,' and your 'no,' 'no'; anything
more than that is from the Evil One." (Mt 5:33–37)*

What does the eighth commandment require of us?

The eighth commandment requires us to be truthful and
to interpret in the best possible way the actions of others. Our
truthfulness bears witness to our belief that God is Truth.
(2464)

*Therefore, put away falsehood and let everyone speak the truth to
his neighbor, because we are parts of one another. (Eph 4:25)*

How do we show our loyalty as disciples?

We show our loyalty to Christ as disciples by bearing witness to the truth, by living up to the Gospel and by willingly

sharing our faith with others. Should circumstances ever require it, we should also be ready to offer the supreme witness of martyrdom rather than deny Christ. (2471–2474)

> *So Pilate said to him, "So you are a king?" Jesus answered, "You say that I am a king. For this I was born and for this I came into the world—to bear witness to the truth. Everyone who is of the truth hears my voice." (Jn 18:37)*

Why is truthfulness important?

Truthfulness is important for our own integrity, for trust and understanding among people, and for our loyalty to Christ as disciples. (2467–2470)

> *If we say we are in fellowship with him yet walk in darkness we are lying and do not follow the truth. . . . (1 Jn 1:6)*

What does the eighth commandment forbid?

The eighth commandment forbids lying, rash judgments, perjury, false witness, rash suspicions, detraction, calumny, talebearing, and telling secrets we are bound to keep.

> *So lay aside all malice and deceit, all hypocrisy, envy, and slander. (1 Pt 2:1)*

What is a lie?

A lie is an untruth said for the purpose of deceiving others. (2482–2483)

> *Do not lie to one another. (Col 3:9)*

Will a good reason for telling a lie excuse it?

No reason, however good, will excuse telling a lie, because a lie is always bad in itself. It is never allowed, even for a good intention, to do a thing that is bad in itself. A lie offends against justice, charity, and trust. (2483–2487)

What is a jocose lie?

A jocose lie is a story made up for the purpose of amusing or instructing others. It becomes sinful if the person telling it does not make it clear that it must not be taken literally.

What is a mental reservation?

A mental reservation, made in circumstances when one is bound in conscience not to tell the entire truth, limits the sense of the speaker's words to a certain meaning. To make a complete reservation to the truth is a lie. (2488–2489)

What is perjury?

Perjury is to lie while under an oath to be truthful. Perjury committed in a court of law can cause grave injustice and injury to innocent persons and can result in legal action against the perjurer. (2476)

A false witness will not go unpunished. (Prov 19:9)

What is rash judgment?

Rash judgment is believing, without sufficient reason, something harmful to another's character. (2477)

What is detraction?

Detraction is making known, without good reason, the hidden faults of others. (2477)

What is slander or calumny?

Slander or calumny is to injure the good name of another by lying. (2477–2479)

You shall not go around as a slanderer among your people. (Lev 19:16 NRSV)

What is talebearing?

Talebearing is telling persons what others have said about them, especially if the things said are evil. It is wrong because it gives rise to anger, hatred, and ill-will, and often causes greater sins.

Do not be called double-tongued and do not lay traps with your tongue. (Sir 5:14 NRSV)

How can flattery and adulation be sinful?

Flattery and adulation (groveling) can be sinful if they are used to encourage or praise another's wrongdoing. (2480)

A lying tongue hates its victims, and a flattering mouth works ruin. (Prov 26:28)

Are there other offenses to truthfulness?

Boasting or bragging offends the truth by inflating our own importance or good qualities. Irony also is an offense when it seeks to take away from the goodness of others or from the worth of their achievements. (2481)

When are we obliged to keep a secret?

We are obliged to keep a secret when we have promised to do so, when our office requires it, or when the good of others demands it. (2492)

Whoever betrays secrets destroys confidence, and will never find a congenial friend. (Sir 27:16)

Is sacramental confession a secret?

Yes, the priest may never reveal anything that is said in sacramental confession, which is a sacred secret. To break this seal of secrecy for any reason is a serious sin. (2490)

Is it ever permitted to read others' letters or private writings?

These may never be read without permission (even reasonably presumed) from the owner, unless the motive is to prevent grave harm to oneself, to another person, or to society.

What must a person do who has sinned in any of these ways?

A person who has sinned in any of these ways against charity and justice must intend to repair the harm done to his neighbor. The reparation should be public if at all possible, but if necessary it may be made privately. (2487)

Why do individuals and society have a right to information?

Society needs information in order to make right decisions, and well-informed citizens contribute to the common good.

Is the right to the communication of truth unconditional?

This right is not unconditional but is governed by love of neighbor as the Gospel teaches. Charity remains the greatest good. (2488)

What other rights parallel the right to information?

Other rights that parallel the right to information are the right to privacy for individuals, families, and societies, as well as the right of secrecy, which is binding for professional reasons and for matters of conscience. (2489–2492)

What are the responsibilities of mass media professionals?

They must be acquainted with the norms of morality and conscientiously practice them in this area. They must always give what is true and, as far as justice and charity permit, what is complete. This calls for balanced judgment and prudence. (2494)

How should readers, listeners, and viewers use the media?

Readers, listeners, and viewers should critically evaluate media presentations and choose what is morally good and truthful. Parents are to train their children in the responsible use of the media. (2496)

How is public opinion justly promoted?

Spreading information that serves the truth, recognizes human dignity, and benefits all is a sure and just way to form public opinion.

What role do civil authorities have in the media?

Civil authorities have the right and the duty to insure freedom of information. They must also be vigilant concerning the abuse of this freedom. Neither governments nor other parties should use the media to manipulate public opinion through disinformation. (2498–2499)

How are education and the media related?

The media, an excellent means of reaching the greatest number of people in the most effective way, should be used to educate humanity. Media presentations should encourage people to reflect upon what they see and to share their experiences with others, all for the common good.

Is it permissible to manipulate information obtained from digital media?

It is not permitted to manipulate information of a private or public nature obtained from digital media. Stealing information or hacking personal or public computers in order to illegally use or misuse the information obtained is sinful. Personal computers and all other digital media are subject to ethical behavior.

What is truth in advertising?

Truth in advertising means that vendors can make known the benefits of their products and services, provided the individual's freedom of choice is respected and the truth is not distorted or hidden.

Is beauty a form of truth?

Beauty is truth made visible. The Bible tells us how God expressed his Truth in creating the universe, and expressed his own image in creating the human person. We, too, using our God-given talents, express the beauty of truth in our art forms. In sacred art we intend to honor God and to gather others to him in adoration and praise. (2500–2502)

Ninth Commandment

What is the ninth commandment of God?

The ninth commandment of God is:

You shall not covet your neighbor's wife. (Ex 20:17)

What did Jesus say about the ninth commandment?

Jesus said:

"I say to you that anyone who looks at a woman with lust for her has already committed adultery with her in his heart." (Mt 5:28)

What is covetousness?

In theology, covetousness, or concupiscence, refers to intense desires in which our feelings are stronger than our reason. This disorder, stemming from original sin, creates a constant tension or pull between the flesh and the spirit. (2514–2516)

But I tell you, walk according to the Spirit, and do not carry out the desires of the flesh. For the flesh's desires are opposed to the Spirit, and the Spirit is opposed to the flesh. (Gal 5:16–17)

What does the ninth commandment require of us?

The ninth commandment requires us to be pure in thoughts and desires. This calls for practice of the virtue of temperance. (2517)

But the things that come from the mouth come from the heart, and those are the things that make a man unclean. For from the heart come wicked thoughts. (Mt 15:18–19)

What does the ninth commandment forbid?

The ninth commandment forbids impure thoughts, sought or entertained with pleasure, impure imaginings voluntarily excited or not rejected, and evil desires.

What is purity of heart?

The sixth beatitude says, "Blessed are the pure of heart, for they shall see God." Those who practice this beatitude keep their mind and will focused on the love of God in their hearts. They already see God in all persons and situations and try to make God seen in their lives. (2518–2519)

Beloved, we are now God's children, but it is not yet clear what we will be. We know that when [Jesus] appears we will be like him, because we will see him as he is. Everyone who has this hope in him purifies himself, just as he is pure. (1 Jn 3:2–3)

How can one grow in purity of heart?

The virtue of chastity helps us to love others sincerely, respecting them as persons. Purity of intention guides us to seek God's will in everything. Prayer, especially the sacraments

of Penance and Eucharist, along with a devotion to the Blessed
Virgin, gives us the strength to grow in this virtue. It also
requires self-discipline and good judgment in avoiding whatever might be a source of temptation. Appreciation for the gift
of sexuality leads us to use it only in the way God intended.
(2520–2521)

> *May God fill you with the knowledge of his will through wisdom
> and all manner of spiritual understanding that you may conduct
> yourselves in a manner worthy of the Lord and fully pleasing to
> him. . . .* (Col 1:9–10)

What is modesty?

Modesty is a virtue that inclines us to guard our senses so
as to avoid possible temptations. It also helps us to refrain from
whatever might incite others to sin, and to be proper in dress
and behavior. It is the temperate guardian of our chastity.
(2521–2524)

Does the question of online pornography come under the ninth commandment?

Yes, the growing interest and often addiction to online
pornography websites is a matter of the ninth commandment.
Those who visit these sites are opening themselves to temptation against their own dignity and the responsibilities of their
state in life, e.g., their marital and familial responsibilities.

Are all unchaste temptations sinful?

Temptations against the sixth and ninth commandments
are not sinful in themselves, but they should not be deliberately stirred up. They only become sinful when unchaste
thoughts, desires, or passions are deliberately aroused and willingly consented to or indulged in.

Tenth Commandment

What is the tenth commandment of God?

The tenth commandment of God is:

You shall not covet your neighbor's house . . . or his manservant, or his maidservant, or his ox, or his ass, or anything that is your neighbor's. (Ex 20:17)

What did Jesus say about the tenth commandment?

Jesus said:

"For where your treasure is, there will your heart be too." (Mt 6:21)

What does the tenth commandment require of us?

The tenth commandment requires that we be satisfied with what is ours and respect the possessions of others.

What does the tenth commandment forbid?

The tenth commandment forbids greed, avarice, and even the desire to obtain unjustly what belongs to another. (2534, 2536)

Those who want to be rich fall into temptations and snares, into many foolish and harmful desires which plunge them into destruction and ruin. For love of money is the root of all evil. (1 Tm 6:9–10)

What is envy?

Envy is a capital sin that produces sadness because of another's possessions and the strong desire to unjustly acquire them. (2538–2539)

Love is patient, love is kind, it is not jealous, does not boast, is not arrogant. (1 Cor 13:4)

Is the sin of envy the same as feeling a desire for what is not ours?

The sin of envy is a deliberate act of the will, while a desire for what is not ours may arise from a spontaneous feeling that is not in itself sinful. These feelings should not be cultivated so as to result in envy. (2541–2543)

Those who belong to Christ have crucified the flesh with its passions and desires. (Gal 5:24)

What is poverty of heart?

Poverty of heart is a detachment from material goods and a disposition for the goods of God's kingdom. All one's affections, desires, and efforts are set on God who is preferred above everything. (2544–2546)

So in the same way, no one who does not part with all his possessions can be my disciple. (Lk 14:33)

What is our ultimate desire?

All our desires for goods and happiness point us toward the vision and blessedness of God, who is the true longing of the human heart. (2548–2550)

When everything is made subject to him, then the Son himself will be subjected to the one who subjected everything to the Son, so that God will be all in all. (1 Cor 15:28)

Some Special Duties of Catholic Christians

Does the Catholic Church have the right to make laws?

The Catholic Church has the right to make laws from its founder, Jesus Christ, who said to the apostles, his first leaders, and bishops:

I will give you the keys to the kingdom of heaven, and whatever
you bind on earth will have been bound in heaven, and whatever
you loose on earth will have been loosed in heaven. (Mt 16:19)

Who exercises the Church's right to make laws?

The Pope and bishops united with him exercise the
Church's right to make laws. The Pope has complete, supreme,
ordinary, and immediate jurisdiction over the universal Church.
(880, 882, 883, 886)

When else may laws be made that affect the universal Church?

Laws that affect the universal Church may be made by a
general council of bishops united with the Pope, as at the
Second Vatican Council. (884)

What are the precepts of the Church?

The precepts of the Church are special duties that Catholics
are expected to obey and fulfill. These precepts prescribe
certain acts of religion and penance, in order to apply the commandments of God and the teachings of the Gospel to the
lives of the faithful. (2041)

What is the purpose of these precepts?

These precepts, which are laws made by the Church, guarantee that Catholics practice the minimum amount of prayer
and penance to grow in love of God and our neighbor. (2041)

What are these special duties of Catholics, called the precepts of the Church?

Some duties expected of Catholics today include the
following:

1. To worship God by participating in Mass every Sunday and holy day of obligation in order to keep holy the day of the Lord's resurrection, and to rest from servile labor on these days. (2042)

2. To receive the sacrament of Reconciliation at least once a year; this continues the work of conversion in preparation for reception of the Eucharist. (2042)

3. To receive Holy Communion during the Easter season (in the United States and Canada, this duty may be fulfilled between the first Sunday of Lent to Trinity Sunday); this guarantees reception of the Body and Blood of the Lord at the Paschal time, which is the heart of the Church's liturgy. (2042)

4. To observe the days of fasting and abstinence established by the Church. These penitential acts prepare us for the feasts of the liturgical year, as well as strengthen us spiritually. (2043)

5. To help to provide for the needs of the Church. This means that the faithful are to assist with the material needs of the Church, according to their ability. (2043)

What are the holy days of obligation in the United States?

Besides all Sundays of the year, canon law specifies ten holy days of obligation, but allows the bishops of each country to determine if they will be observed as holy days of obligation. In the United States, the holy days are:

- ❖ January 1, Solemnity of Mary, Mother of God;
- ❖ Ascension of Our Lord (forty days after Easter, or in some dioceses, the following Sunday);
- ❖ August 15, Assumption of the Blessed Virgin Mary;
- ❖ November 1, All Saints' Day;
- ❖ December 8, Immaculate Conception of Mary;
- ❖ December 25, Christmas Day.

Note: Christmas is always a holy day of obligation on whatever day it falls. When the feasts of the Assumption, All Saints, or the Solemnity of Mary, Mother of God (January 1) are celebrated on a Saturday or Monday, there is no obligation to participate in Mass. The Immaculate Conception remains a holy day of obligation except when December 8 falls on Sunday. Then the feast is transferred to Monday, in which case it is not considered a holy day. However, the faithful are still encouraged to participate at Mass on these days.

The other holy days specified in canon law for the universal Church are: Epiphany, Corpus Christi (The Body and Blood of the Lord), the feasts of St. Joseph (March 19) and the Apostles Peter and Paul (June 29). (2177) (See also pages 195–197 for the section on Sunday Mass under the third commandment.)

What are the holy days celebrated in Canada?

Catholics in Canada celebrate two holy days of obligation: Christmas Day and the Feast of Mary, Mother of God. Epiphany, Ascension of the Lord, and Corpus Christi are transferred to the following Sunday.

What does Church law say about penance?

All Catholics are bound to do some penance in virtue of divine law. So that all may be joined in a common observance of penance, penitential days are prescribed in which the faithful pray, perform good works, deny themselves by fulfilling their responsibilities more faithfully, and observe fast and abstinence. (1434–1435, 1438, 2043)

> *But the days will come when the bridegroom will be taken from them, and then, on that day, they will fast.* (Mk 2:20)

What is a fast day?

A fast day is a day in which only one full meal is taken; the other two meals together should not equal a full meal. In the United States and Canada, the only fast days are Ash Wednesday and Good Friday. Eating between meals is not permitted, but liquids, including milk and fruit juices, are allowed. (1438)

Why has the Church instituted fast days?

The Church has instituted fast days so that we Christians may learn to set our sights on God and the goal of our human life by self-denial. This is to follow the example of Jesus. (540, 2043)

> Then Jesus was led into the desert by the Spirit to be tempted by the Devil. After fasting for forty days and forty nights he at last became hungry. (Mt 4:1–2)

Who are obliged to fast?

Catholics who have reached the age of eighteen but are not yet fifty-nine are obliged to fast.

What does the law of abstinence mean?

The law of abstinence means refraining from eating meat on certain "days of abstinence" stipulated by the Church, such as Ash Wednesday.

In the United States what are the days for abstinence from meat?

In the United States the days for abstinence from meat are Ash Wednesday, the Fridays of Lent, and Good Friday. Catholics fourteen years of age and over are obliged to keep this law.

In Canada what are the days for abstinence from meat?

In Canada the days for abstinence from meat are Ash Wednesday and Good Friday. All other Fridays, including the Fridays of Lent, are days of abstinence, but Catholics may substitute abstinence with some other act of piety or charity. Catholics fourteen years of age and over are obliged to keep this law.

Are fasting and abstinence the only penances required of Catholics?

Fasting and abstinence are not the only penances required by Catholics. We are to do more penances of our own choosing especially on Fridays throughout the year, since Jesus gave his life for us on a Friday, and during Lent, when we recall what the Lord suffered for us.

CHRISTIAN PRAYER

Prayer: Communication with God

What is prayer?

Prayer is talking to God with mind and heart, and often with the voice. It is a response to God's invitation to seek him. (2559)

Come to me, all you grown weary and burdened, and I will refresh you. (Mt 11:28)

Why do we pray in the name of Christ?

Through Baptism we are one with Christ and his Church; therefore, all our prayers are offered with him to the Father in the Holy Spirit. (2565)

In Christ we have free and confident access to God through our faith in him. (Eph 3:12)

Must everyone pray?

God calls every person to prayer. He wants to engage us in a personal relationship, a conversation. Even if some do not hear the call nor pay attention to it, God continues his invitation to each human heart. (2566–2567)

By groping about after him they might search for and find God, for he is not far from any of us. (Acts 17:27)

How can we learn to pray?

We learn to pray best by praying, by talking to God from our own heart. Many examples of prayer can be found throughout the pages of Scripture, especially in the Psalms. (2568–2619, 2653–2654)

> *Give ear to my words, O LORD; give heed to my sighing. Listen to the sound of my cry, my King and my God, for to you do I pray. O LORD, in the morning you hear my voice; in the morning I plead my case to you, and watch.* (Ps 5:1–3)

How should we pray?

We should pray with the same sentiments that the Gospels demonstrate:

- ❖ conversion of heart (Mt 5:23–24)
- ❖ faith (Mt 7:7–11)
- ❖ filial boldness (Mk 9:23)
- ❖ desire to do God's will (Mt 9:38)
- ❖ watchfulness (Mk 1:15)
- ❖ perseverance (Lk 11:5–13)
- ❖ patience (Lk 18:1–8)
- ❖ humility (Lk 18:9–14) (2607–2613)

What are the types of prayer?

These are the types of prayer:
- ❖ blessing (Eph 1:3)
- ❖ adoration (Ps 95:6)
- ❖ petition (Col 4:12)
- ❖ asking forgiveness (Lk 18:13)
- ❖ intercession (1 Tm 2:1)
- ❖ thanksgiving (1 Thes 5:18)
- ❖ praise (Eph 3:20) (2626–2643)

What are the best sources of prayer?

The best sources of prayer are God's Word (Scripture), the Church's liturgy (prayers and sacraments), and the virtues of faith, hope, and love (dispositions to prayer). (2653–2658)

When should we pray?

We should pray every day, and we can pray at any time, in any circumstance, for any reason. (2659–2660, 2742)

Pray at all times in the Spirit with every manner of prayer and supplication. (Eph 6:18)

Where can we learn to pray?

The main school of prayer is the family, where Christian beliefs and practices are explained and shared. The Church's liturgy, along with her ministers and teachers, also offer us opportunities to learn how to pray. Religious congregations share their spirituality with others, and we can also learn prayer from the lives and writings of the saints. (2683–2690)

Anyone who lives on milk is still a child and is inexperienced in the word of righteousness, whereas solid food is for the mature. (Heb 5:13–14)

For whom should we pray?

We should pray for ourselves, our family, relatives, friends and neighbors, the Pope, bishops, priests and religious, government leaders, lawmakers, judges and public officials, the sick and the dying, sinners, unbelievers, the unborn, the suffering souls in purgatory, and even for our enemies.

First of all, I urge that supplications, prayers, intercessions and thanksgivings be made for all men—for kings and for all those in positions of authority. (1 Tm 2:1–2)

What are the common forms of prayer?

Three common forms of prayer are vocal prayer, meditation, and contemplative prayer. (2721)

What is vocal prayer?

Vocal prayer is prayer of mind, heart, and lips. It is prayer spoken audibly. (2700–2704)

> O LORD, *open my lips, and my mouth will declare your praise.* (Ps 51:15)

What is meditation?

Meditation is a mental (unspoken) prayer in which a person, after quiet reflection, arrives at or strengthens a resolution to live a better Christian life. Meditation can lead us to know Jesus better and follow him more closely. (2705–2708)

> *Reflect on the statutes of the* LORD, *and meditate at all times on his commandments. It is he who will give insight to your mind, and your desire for wisdom will be granted.* (Sir 6:37)

What is contemplative prayer?

Contemplative (mental) prayer is unspoken prayer in which a person is united to God and ponders his truths. (2709–2719)

> *Then there are those sown on the good earth, who are the ones who hear the word and welcome it and bear fruit, one thirtyfold, one sixtyfold, and one a hundredfold.* (Mk 4:20)

Why are we often distracted during prayer?

Worries, anxieties, or physical discomfort can distract us, while other distractions may come from the devil. The efforts we make to overcome these distractions make our prayer better and more pleasing to God. (2729)

What other difficulties can affect our prayer?

False expectations, lack of feeling, disinterest, laziness, or weak faith can also make our prayer difficult. (2726–2728, 2730–2733)

If the grain of wheat that falls to the ground does not die, it remains alone, but if it dies, it bears much fruit. (Jn 12:24)

Why do we not always obtain what we pray for?

God knows what is best for us, and can see that a particular request may not be for our ultimate good. In these cases he gives us some other spiritual gift according to his loving plan for our lives. Every sincere prayer is answered in some way. (2735–2737)

This is the confidence we have in [God], that if we ask for something which is in accordance with his will he hears us. (1 Jn 5:14)

How can we pray better?

We can pray better by allowing the Holy Spirit to pray in us, remembering that prayer is the duty and privilege of a Christian. (2745)

Pray at all times in the Spirit with every manner of prayer and supplication. (Eph 6:18)

Why is it important to pray at times with others?

It is important to pray at times with others because Jesus wants us to come to prayer as a community.

For where two or three are gathered in my name, I am there among them. (Mt 18:20)

What is the greatest community prayer?

The greatest community prayer is the Mass. (See the section on the Eucharist, pages 96-116.)

What is the Sign of the Cross?

The Sign of the Cross is a prayer that reminds us of two important mysteries of our faith: the Blessed Trinity and the redemption. As the prayer is said, the cross is traced from our forehead to our chest and from the left shoulder to the right shoulder. We are literally "signing" ourselves with the cross.

How are the mysteries of the Trinity and redemption expressed in the Sign of the Cross?

When we say "In the name," we express the truth that there is one God. When we say, "of the Father, and of the Son, and of the Holy Spirit," we manifest our belief that there are three distinct Persons in God. When we make the form of the cross on ourselves, we express our belief that the Son of God-made-man redeemed us by his death on the cross.

When do we usually make the sign of the cross?

We usually make the sign of the cross when we begin and end our prayers and when we enter and leave a church.

What are some prayers that every Catholic is encouraged to know by heart?

Some prayers that every Catholic may want to know by heart are the Our Father, the Hail Mary, the Apostles' Creed, the Glory, the Hail Holy Queen, the Angel of God, the Eternal Rest for the souls in purgatory; the acts of faith, hope, love, and contrition; the morning offering; and grace before and after meals.

The Lord's Prayer

Why is the Lord's Prayer considered a perfect prayer?

The Lord's Prayer is considered a perfect prayer principally because it comes from Jesus himself. It serves as a model for all prayer because it offers worship and praise to the Father and accurately states our human needs. We can pray together or privately contemplate this perfect prayer for all occasions. (2761–2766)

Why is the Lord's Prayer found in the Mass?

The Lord's Prayer is appropriate in the Mass because it summarizes all the petitions and intentions of the Eucharistic liturgy. It also directs our attention to the Lord's return at the end of time. (2770–2772)

For whenever you eat this bread and drink this cup you proclaim the death of the Lord, until he comes. (1 Cor 11:26)

What is the importance of calling God our Father?

Because we are used to calling God our Father, it is easy to overlook the uniqueness of this privilege. Jesus has invited us to join in his intimate relationship with his "Abba." The awe and fear we naturally feel toward our Creator God is modified by the confidence and boldness of a loved child. (2777–2778)

The Spirit itself bears witness with our spirit that we are God's children. (Rom 8:16)

What does this relationship require of us?

This relationship with God as Father requires of us a gratitude expressed in humility and a desire to live the new life offered in Christ. (2779–2785)

Whoever humbles himself like this child . . . is the greatest in the kingdom of heaven. (Mt 18:4)

Where is God's heaven?

When we pray to "Our Father who art in heaven," we are addressing God in his transcendence. God is the Being from which everything else receives being; he is above all other beings in majesty and power. Heaven is not a place, but the presence of God. We will find our eternal home in him. (2794–2796)

Here we groan, because we long to put on our heavenly dwelling. . . . (2 Cor 5:2)

What does it mean to "hallow"?

When we pray that God's name may be hallowed, we are praying to enter into his holy plan: that by our lives, work, and prayers, his holiness may be recognized and glorified. (2807–2815)

Consecrate yourselves therefore, and be holy, for I am holy. (Lev 11:44)

When will God's kingdom come?

God's kingdom will come when the world as we know it has ended, and we are all taken up into his eternal reign. We must try to make God the King of the here and now. (2816–2821)

Therefore, do not let sin reign in your mortal bodies so that you obey bodily desires . . . instead, offer yourselves to God. (Rom 6:12–13)

What is God's will?

God's will is that we keep the commandment of love toward him and all people, that all may be saved. (2822–2827)

> *He made known to us the mystery of his will, according to the purpose he displayed in Christ as a plan for the fullness of time—to bring all things together in Christ, things in the heavens and things on earth.* (Eph 1:9–10)

What do we pray for in asking for our daily bread?

When we pray for our daily bread, we are asking for the food and care we need in this life, but also for the Eucharist, the heavenly Bread. (2828–2837)

> *Labor not for food that perishes, but for food that remains for life eternal. . . .* (Jn 6:27)

What are trespasses?

Trespasses are anything we do against another, that is, our sins or offenses. In the Lord's Prayer we ask God to forgive all that we have done wrong, in the same way that we are forgiving toward others who wrong us. (2838–2845)

> *Be kind to one another, compassionate, forgiving each other just as God forgave you in Christ.* (Eph 4:32)

Does God tempt us?

No, God does not tempt us but may sometimes allow trials that lead to our spiritual growth. We ask him to deliver us from poor judgment, bad decisions, and weakness in face of evil. (2846–2849)

> *The only temptations you have received are normal human ones. God is trustworthy and will not allow you to be tested beyond your strength—along with the temptation he will also provide a way out, so you will be able to endure it.* (1 Cor 10:13)

Will God protect us against the devil?

Yes, and he already has in the victory Jesus won on the cross. We must stay close to Jesus because the devil, the evil angel, is always looking for an opportunity to deceive us. (2850–2854)

> *I do not pray for you to take them out of the world, but for you to preserve them from the Evil One.* (Jn 17:15)

What does "amen" mean?

"Amen" means "I agree with that," "May it be as you have said." (2856)

> *Let it be done to me according to your word.* (Lk 1:38)

The Hail Mary and the Rosary

Where did the Hail Mary come from?

The first part of the Hail Mary consists of the greetings which the angel and Elizabeth addressed to Mary, as recorded in the Gospel; the second part was added by the Church as our response under the guidance of the Holy Spirit. (2676–2677)

> *And when he [the angel] came into her presence he said, "Hail, full of grace, the Lord is with you!"* (Lk 1:28)

> *[Elizabeth] exclaimed with a loud cry, "Blessed are you among women, and blessed is the fruit of your womb!"* (Lk 1:42)

Should we often pray the Hail Mary?

Yes, because the Hail Mary recalls the Incarnation of the Son of God for our salvation, honors Mary as the Mother of God, and asks for her help during our life and at the moment of our death.

What is the Rosary?

The Rosary is a "Gospel prayer" made up of the Our Father, Hail Mary, and Glory, in which we meditate on important events in the lives of Jesus and Mary. (2678)

Does the Church recommend praying the Rosary?

The Church and all the recent Popes have highly recommended praying the Rosary to grow in the spiritual life and obtain peace for the world.

APPENDICES

Prayers

The Sign of the Cross

In the name of the Father, and of the Son, and of the Holy Spirit. Amen.

The Lord's Prayer

Our Father, who art in heaven, hallowed be thy name; thy kingdom come; thy will be done on earth as it is in heaven. Give us this day our daily bread, and forgive us our trespasses, as we forgive those who trespass against us, and lead us not into temptation, but deliver us from evil. Amen.

Hail Mary

Hail Mary, full of grace! The Lord is with you. Blessed are you among women, and blessed is the fruit of your womb, Jesus. Holy Mary, Mother of God, pray for us sinners, now and at the hour of our death. Amen.

Glory

Glory to the Father, and to the Son, and to the Holy Spirit. As it was in the beginning, is now, and will be forever. Amen.

The Angelus

The Angel of the Lord declared unto Mary. And she conceived of the Holy Spirit.

Hail Mary . . .

Behold the handmaid of the Lord.

May it be done unto me according to your word.

Hail Mary . . .

And the Word became flesh. And lived among us.

Hail Mary . . .

Pray for us, O Holy Mother of God.

That we may be made worthy of the promises of Christ.

Let us pray. O Lord, it was through the message of an angel that we learned of the Incarnation of your Son Christ. Pour your grace into our hearts, and by his passion and cross bring us to the glory of his resurrection. Through the same Christ, our Lord. Amen.

Glory to the Father . . .

Regina Coeli

Said during the Easter Season instead of the Angelus.

Queen of heaven, rejoice, Alleluia.

For he whom you deserved to bear, Alleluia.

Has risen as he said, Alleluia.

Pray for us to God, Alleluia.

Rejoice and be glad, O Virgin Mary! Alleluia!

Because our Lord is truly risen, Alleluia.

Let us pray. O God, by the resurrection of your Son, our Lord Jesus Christ, you have made glad the whole world. Grant, we pray, that through the intercession of the Virgin Mary, his Mother, we may attain the joys of eternal life. Through Christ our Lord. Amen.

The Apostles' Creed

I believe in God, the Father almighty, Creator of heaven and earth, and in Jesus Christ, his only Son, our Lord, who was conceived by the Holy Spirit, born of the Virgin Mary, suffered under Pontius Pilate, was crucified, died and was buried; he descended into hell; on the third day he rose again from the dead; he ascended into heaven, and is seated at the right hand of God the Father almighty; from there he will come to judge the living and the dead. I believe in the Holy Spirit, the holy catholic Church, the communion of saints, the forgiveness of sins, the resurrection of the body, and life everlasting. Amen.

An Act of Faith

O my God, I firmly believe that you are one God in three divine Persons, Father, Son, and Holy Spirit; I believe that your divine Son became man and died for our sins, and that he will come to judge the living and the dead. I believe these and all the truths which the holy Catholic Church teaches, because you have revealed them, who can neither deceive nor be deceived.

An Act of Hope

O my God, relying on your infinite goodness and promises, I hope to obtain pardon of my sins, the help of your grace, and life everlasting, through the merits of Jesus Christ, my Lord and Redeemer.

An Act of Love

O my God, I love you above all things, with my whole heart and soul, because you are all-good and worthy of all love. I love my neighbor as myself for the love of you. I forgive all who have injured me, and I ask pardon of all whom I have injured.

An Act of Contrition

O my God, I am heartily sorry for having offended you, and I detest all my sins, because of your just punishments, but most of all because they offend you, my God, who are all good and deserving of all my love. I firmly resolve, with the help of your grace, to sin no more and to avoid the near occasions of sin.

Morning Offering

Divine Heart of Jesus, through the Immaculate Heart of Mary, I offer you all my prayers, works, joys, and sufferings of this day, in reparation for sins, and for the salvation of all men and women, according to the special intentions of the Pope, in the grace of the Holy Spirit, for the glory of the heavenly Father. Amen.

Prayer Before Meals

Bless us, O Lord, and these your gifts, which we are about to receive from your bounty, through Christ our Lord. Amen.

Prayer After Meals

We give you thanks for all your benefits, O loving God, you who live and reign forever. Amen.

Prayer Before a Crucifix

Behold, my beloved and good Jesus, I cast myself upon my knees in your sight, and with the most fervent desire of my soul I pray and beseech you to impress upon my heart lively sentiments of faith, hope, and charity, with true repentance for my sins and a most firm desire of amendment; while with deep affection and grief of soul I consider within myself and contemplate your five most precious wounds, having before my eyes that which David, the prophet, long ago spoke about you, my Jesus:

"They have pierced my hands and my feet; I can count all my bones." (Ps 22:17–18)

Hail, Holy Queen

Hail, holy Queen, Mother of mercy, our life, our sweetness, and our hope! To you we cry, poor banished children of Eve; to you we send up our sighs, mourning, and weeping in this valley of tears. Turn then, most gracious advocate, your eyes of mercy toward us, and after this our exile, show unto us the blessed fruit of your womb, Jesus. O clement, O loving, O sweet Virgin Mary.

Memorare

Remember, O most gracious Virgin Mary, that never was it known that anyone who fled to your protection, implored your help, or sought your intercession, was left unaided. Inspired with this confidence, I fly to you, O Virgin of virgins, my Mother; to you I come; before you I kneel, sinful and sorrowful. O Mother of the Word Incarnate, despise not my petitions, but in your mercy hear and answer them. Amen.

How to Pray the Rosary

Note: The complete Rosary consists of twenty decades (a decade is ten beads, upon each is prayed a Hail Mary), divided into four parts of five decades each: the Joyful Mysteries (usually prayed on Mondays and Saturdays), the Luminous Mysteries (Thursdays), the Sorrowful Mysteries (Tuesdays and Fridays), and the Glorious Mysteries (Wednesdays and Sundays).

We begin the Rosary by blessing ourselves with the rosary's crucifix. On the first beads found just after the crucifix, we recite the Apostles' Creed, one Our Father, three Hail Marys, and one Glory on the small chain. Then, on the first set of ten beads, we pray one Our Father, ten Hail Marys, and one Glory. This completes one decade. All the other decades are prayed in the same manner, while meditating on the mystery assigned to each decade. At the end of the Rosary, the Hail Holy Queen and the Litany of the Blessed Virgin Mary may also be recited.

The Mysteries of the Rosary

Joyful Mysteries
1. The Annunciation to the Blessed Virgin Mary
2. Mary Visits Her Cousin Elizabeth
3. The Birth of Jesus at Bethlehem
4. The Presentation of Jesus in the Temple
5. The Finding of the Child Jesus in the Temple

Luminous Mysteries
1. John Baptizes Jesus in the Jordan
2. Jesus Reveals His Glory at the Wedding of Cana
3. Jesus Proclaims the Kingdom of God and Calls Us to Conversion
4. The Transfiguration of Jesus
5. Jesus Gives Us the Eucharist

Sorrowful Mysteries
1. Jesus Prays in the Garden of Gethsemane
2. Jesus Is Scourged at the Pillar
3. Jesus Is Crowned with Thorns
4. Jesus Carries the Cross to Calvary
5. Jesus Dies for Our Sins

Glorious Mysteries
1. Jesus Rises from the Dead
2. Jesus Ascends into Heaven
3. The Holy Spirit Descends on the Apostles and Disciples in the Upper Room
4. Mary Is Assumed into Heaven
5. Mary Is Crowned Queen of Heaven and Earth

Angel of God (or Prayer to My Guardian Angel)

Angel of God, my guardian dear, to whom God's love entrusts me here, ever this day be at my side to light and guard, to rule and guide. Amen.

Eternal Rest

Eternal rest grant to them, O Lord, and let perpetual light shine upon them. May they rest in peace. Amen.

Guidelines for Christian Living

The Ten Commandments of God

I am the Lord your God:

1. You shall not have other gods besides me.
2. You shall not take the name of the Lord your God in vain.
3. Remember to keep holy the Lord's day.
4. Honor your father and your mother.
5. You shall not kill.
6. You shall not commit adultery.
7. You shall not steal.
8. You shall not bear false witness against your neighbor.
9. You shall not covet your neighbor's wife.
10. You shall not covet your neighbor's goods.
    (cf. Ex 20:1–17)

The Two Great Commandments

You shall love the Lord your God with all your heart, with all your soul, with all your mind, and with all your strength.

You shall love your neighbor as yourself.

The Seven Sacraments

Baptism	Anointing of the Sick
Confirmation	Holy Orders
Holy Eucharist	Matrimony
Penance and Reconciliation	

Special Duties of Catholic Christians:
The Precepts of the Church

1. To worship God by participating in Mass every Sunday and holy day of obligation in order to keep holy the day of the Lord's resurrection, and to rest from servile labor on these days.

2. To receive the sacrament of Reconciliation at least once a year; this continues the work of conversion in preparation for reception of the Eucharist.

3. To receive Holy Communion during the Easter season (in the United States and Canada, this duty may be fulfilled between the first Sunday of Lent to Trinity Sunday); this guarantees reception of the Body and Blood of the Lord at the Paschal time, which is the heart of the Church's liturgy.

4. To observe the days of fasting and abstinence established by the Church. These penitential acts prepare us for the feasts of the liturgical year, as well as strengthen us spiritually.

5. To help to provide for the needs of the Church. This means that the faithful are to assist with the material needs of the Church, according to their ability.

The Eight Beatitudes

Blessed are the poor in spirit, for theirs is the kingdom of heaven.

Blessed are those who mourn, for they shall be comforted.

Blessed are the meek, for they shall inherit the earth.

Blessed are those who hunger and thirst to do God's will, for they shall have their fill.

Blessed are the merciful, for they shall receive mercy.

Blessed are the pure of heart, for they shall see God.

Blessed are the peacemakers, for they shall be called sons of God.

Blessed are those who are persecuted for doing God's will, for theirs is the kingdom of heaven.

Blessed are you when they insult you and persecute you and say every sort of evil thing against you on account of me; rejoice and be glad, because your reward will be great in heaven—they persecuted the prophets before you in the same way. (Mt 5:3–12)

The Works of Mercy

Spiritual Works

1. To admonish the sinner.
2. To instruct the ignorant.
3. To counsel the doubtful.
4. To comfort the sorrowful.
5. To bear wrongs patiently.
6. To forgive injuries.
7. To pray for the living and the dead.

Corporal Works

1. To feed the hungry.
2. To give drink to the thirsty.
3. To clothe the naked.
4. To shelter the homeless.
5. To visit the sick.
6. To visit the imprisoned.
7. To bury the dead.

Gifts of the Holy Spirit

Wisdom

Understanding

Counsel (right judgment)

Fortitude (courage)

Knowledge

Piety (love)

Fear of the Lord
(reverence)

Fruits of the Holy Spirit

Charity

Long-suffering

Joy

Humility

Peace

Fidelity

Patience

Modesty

Kindness

Continence

Goodness

Chastity

The Books of the Bible

The Old Testament

Genesis

Exodus

Leviticus

Numbers

Deuteronomy

Joshua

Judges

Ruth

1 Samuel

2 Samuel

1 Kings

2 Kings

1 Chronicles

2 Chronicles

Ezra

Nehemiah

Tobit*

Judith*

Esther

1 Maccabees*

2 Maccabees*

Job

Psalms

Proverbs

Ecclesiastes

Song of Songs

Wisdom*

Sirach*

Isaiah

Jeremiah

Lamentations

Baruch*

Ezekiel

Daniel

Hosea

Joel

Amos

Obadiah

Note: The Catholic Church recognizes those books marked by a star (*) as inspired, but the Protestant tradition does not. However, many Protestant Bibles include them after the Old Testament.

Jonah

Micah

Nahum

Habakkuk

Zephaniah

Haggai

Zechariah

Malachi

The New Testament

Matthew

Mark

Luke

John

Acts of the Apostles

Romans

1 Corinthians

2 Corinthians

Galatians

Ephesians

Philippians

Colossians

1 Thessalonians

2 Thessalonians

1 Timothy

2 Timothy

Titus

Philemon

Hebrews

James

1 Peter

2 Peter

1 John

2 John

3 John

Jude

Revelation or

Apocalypse

Index

A

abortion, 149, 165, 180, 202–3

Abraham, 7, 29

absolution, 118, 120–21, 123

abstinence, 237–240, 265

Adam and Eve, 22–24

addiction, 206, 210, 233

adoration, 74, 102, 186, 231, 244

adultery, 146, 148, 180, 211, 216, 231, 264

Advent, 33, 77–78, 104

agnostics, 189

alb, 112–13

altar, 90, 99, 106, 114, 151, 196

angels, 17–20, 67, 191, 248, 263

Angelus, 257–58

anger, 162, 178, 192, 210, 228

annulment, 144, 148

anointing, 90, 93–94

Anointing of the Sick, 81, 130–33

    effects of, 130–31

    sign of, 130

apostasy, 184

apostles, 9, 39, 46, 51–52, 54, 78, 101, 117, 136

Apostles' Creed, 10, 248

armaments, 209

Ash Wednesday, 153, 239–40

ashes, 66, 152–53

atheists, 4, 88, 189

authorities, civil, 230

authority, 197–200

avarice, 178, 234

B

Baptism, 50, 81, 83–92, 104, 153, 243

    of blood, 86

    and Confirmation, 84, 92, 95

    of desire, 86

    effects of, 11, 83–85

    of infants, 86–87

    minister of, 88–89

    necessity of, 85–87

    seal of, 84

    sign of, 84–85

    and sin, 83, 85

baptistry, 89

beatific vision, 67

Beatitudes, 159–60, 232, 265–66

beauty, 21, 76, 231

Benedict XV, 57

Benedict XVI, 109

Benediction, Eucharistic, 112, 137

Bible. *See* Scripture

birth control. *See* contraception

bishops, 46, 48–49, 51, 53, 92–93, 121, 128, 134–39, 235–36

    college of, 54, 136

    role, of 54–56, 136

blasphemy, 179–80, 192

Blessed Trinity, 13–15

    See also God as Trinity of Persons

blesseds, 67

blessings, 102, 150–53, 244

body. *See* human body

breaking of the bread. *See* Fraction of the Bread

bribe, 220

C

calumny, 226–27

Cana, 36, 140

candles, 89, 114, 133, 152–53

canon law, 56–57, 63, 237–38

capital punishment, 208

cardinals, 54

catechumens, 85

Catholic Church. *See* Church

Catholic faith, 49, 88, 96, 105

    truth of, 49

Catholics, 65, 85

    duties of, 94, 96, 110–11, 235–40

    and family planning, 214–15

    and marriage, 141–49

celibacy, 138–39, 157

cemetery, 65

chalice, 115

chancery office, 56

character (sacramental)

    of Baptism, 84

    of Confirmation, 95

    of Holy Orders, 137–38

charity, 169, 171–73, 186

chastity, 61, 169, 173, 187, 211–18, 232–33

    sins against, 212–13

chasuble, 77, 112–13

cheating, 219

child abuse, 217

children, 148–49

    and divorce, 216

    and love for parents, 197–99

Chosen People, 7, 134

Chrism, 90, 92, 94

Christ. *See* Jesus Christ

Christian prayer, 243–53

Christian name, 91, 194

Christians, 158

Christmas, 77, 237–38

Church

    and Bible, 8–10

    Catholic, 48–64

    as Christ's body, 50, 62

    and college of bishops, 54, 136

    history of, 64

    holiness of, 51, 79

    and Holy Spirit, 48–49

    and indulgences, 127–29

    and Jesus, 48, 50, 52, 55, 57

    laws of, 163, 195–96, 235–40

    and liturgy, 75–78

    Magisterium of, 55–56

    marks of, 50–51

      apostolicity of, 51

      catholicity of, 51

      holiness of, 51, 79

      unity of, 50, 63

    members of, 48

    mission of, 57, 59–60

    mystery of, 48–52

    as Mystical Body, 50, 81, 129

    nature of, 49

    necessity of, 51

    People of God, 48–50

    and Pope, 48, 52–58, 236

    role of laity, 57–8

    as sacrament of salvation, 48, 81

    and sacramentals, 150–54

    and sacraments, 81

      Anointing, 130–33

      Baptism, 83–92

      Confirmation, 92–96

      Eucharist, 95–116

      Penance, 117–124

      Holy Orders, 134–39

      Matrimony, 139–49

    and salvation history, 28

    and social teaching, 220–24

    teaching authority of, 5–6, 169, 217

    and Vatican II, 49, 109, 236

ciborium, 115

cincture, 113

citizens, 200

clergy scandal, 136, 204

Collect, 103–4

commandment, greatest, 159, 171

communion of saints, 62–63

Communion Rite, 108

Concluding doxology, 108

Concluding Rites of the Mass, 108

confession. *See* Penance and Reconciliation

confessor, 121–2, 165

Confirmation, 81, 92–6
    and Baptism, 84, 92, 95
    effects of, 94
    minister of, 92
    necessity of, 95
    preparation for, 96
    seal of, 84
    sign of, 93
    sponsor, 96

conjugal love, 145, 148

conscience, 158, 163–66, 182, 199, 209, 217
    examination of, 119, 124–27

consecrated life, 60–62, 141

consecrated virgin, 62

contemplation, 246

contraception, 149, 214–15

contrition, 86, 118–19, 186, 259

corporal, 115

Corpus Christi, 99, 238

counsel, 172

covenant, 7–8, 28, 35, 140, 145, 181, 195, 216

covetousness, 231–35

creation, 16–24, 221, 224

Creed, 10, 105, 129

cremains, 66

cremation, 65–66, 207

crucifix, 114, 128, 152–53, 260

cruets, 115

cursing, 192

D

dalmatic, 113

David, 7, 35

deacons, 134, 136–37

death, 65, 201–9

deposit of faith, 6

despair, 179, 184–85

detraction, 227

Deuteronomy, 181

devil, 19, 90, 188, 246, 252

devotion, 32, 60, 76–77, 150

diaconate, 136–37

digital media, manipulation, 230

diocese, 56

disciples, 39, 225–26

discipleship, 160

disparity of cult, 144

dispensation, 144–45, 188

divine inspiration, 7, 9

divorce, 145–48, 216

Doctors of the Church, 9

drug abuse, 206, 210

drunkenness, 210

dying, the, 204, 207

E

Easter, 10, 41, 43, 77–78, 90

Easter duty, 110–11

Eastern Orthodox, 58

Eastern Rites, 58, 92, 95, 138, 142

ecumenical council, 55

ecumenism, 58

embryo, human, 203–4

employers, 222

encyclical, 53

end of the world, 71–72

envy, 178, 185, 234–35

Epiphany, 36, 238

eternal life, 26, 65–72, 158

Eucharist, 26, 43, 81, 95–116, 251

    consecration of, 97–98, 115

    effects of, 97, 102, 109

    and fasting, 110

    and Holy Communion, 108, 196–97, 237

    and Last Supper, 100

    and other Christians, 111

    preparation for, 109

    and Real Presence, 97–99, 112

    reception of, 99, 110–11, 122, 128, 133

    reverence for, 76, 112

    type of bread and wine used, 114–15

Eucharistic Celebration, 99–109, 186, 247, 249

    celebrant of, 102

    names for, 100

    purpose of, 99–103

    rites of, 103–8

    and sacrifice of cross, 101, 103

    and Sunday obligation, 103, 110, 194–97

Eucharistic devotion, 76, 111–12

Eucharistic ministers, 133

Eucharistic Prayer, 107

euthanasia, 202–4

evangelical counsels, 60–61

evangelization, 59

evil spirits, 151

evolution, 21

ex cathedra, 53

excommunication, 63, 121, 203

Exodus, 181

Exorcism, 151

Extraordinary Form of the Mass, 109

F

faith, 10, 29, 169–70, 184, 186, 244

    sins against, 184

faithful, 11, 57, 61

    priesthood of, 135

faithfulness, 173

family, 149, 197–200, 212, 214, 245

fasting, 110, 238–39

Fathers of the Church, 9, 17

fear of the Lord, 172–73

fidelity, 7, 145, 212, 214

finger towel, 116

flattery, 228

forgiveness, 117–18

fornication, 212–13

fortitude, 167–68, 172–73

Fraction of the Bread, 108

free union, 217

freedom, 4, 20, 22 161, 167
    religious, 188

fundamental option, 180

funerals, 65, 137

G

Gabriel, 19, 29, 33

gambling, 224

generosity, 173

genocide, 209

gentleness, 173

Gloria, 103–4

gluttony, 178

God
    attributes of, 12–13
    Creator, 3–4, 16–17, 183
    existence of, 3–4
    and forgiveness of sins, 118

God the Father, 14, 16, 249

God the Holy Spirit, 14, 45–47

God the Son, 14, 28–44, 249
    holiness of, 79
    knowledge of, 3, 25
    love of, 26, 125, 171–72, 185
    and marriage, 139
    mercy of, 12
    and name YHWH, 13, 190, 250
    nature of, 12
    and our eternal destiny, 3, 15, 27, 157
    perfection of, 12
    prayer, 243–53
    Providence of, 13, 20
    and redemption, 39–40
    service of, 26
    and sin, 164, 175–80
    as source of human happiness, 25
    as Trinity of Persons, 13–15, 247–48
    will of, 86, 150, 164, 170, 232, 244, 251
    worship of, 4, 76, 183–90, 237

godparents, 90–91, 96, 198

Good Friday, 41, 239–40

Good News, 29, 85

goodness, 173

Gospels, 33

    authors, 8–9

    and divinity of Christ, 8

    historicity of, 4

grace, 22, 39, 43–44, 46–47, 83, 86, 161, 171, 176, 182

    sacramental, 80

Greeting (at Mass), 103–4

H

Hail Mary, 154, 248, 253, 257

happiness, 25, 235

hatred, 210, 228

health, 130–33, 150, 205–7

heaven, 27, 66–69, 250

hell, 41, 66, 69–70, 72

heresy, 184

heritage of faith, 6

hermit, 62

hierarchy. *See* bishops

holiness, 79

Holy Communion. *See* Eucharist

holy days, 77, 103, 194, 237–38

Holy Orders, 81, 84, 134–39, 187

    degrees of, 136–38

    sign of, 137–38

    and women, 138

Holy Spirit, 45–47, 53

    and anointing, 131

    and the Church, 5, 9, 46, 48–49, 55

    and Confirmation, 92–96

    and contrition, 121

    divinity of, 45

    and faith, 29

    fruits of, 173, 267

    gifts of, 83, 172–73, 267

    and grace, 83, 47, 158, 164

    and Holy Orders, 137, 139

    and inspiration, 7

    Paraclete, 45

    and Pentecost, 46

    and sacraments, 79–80, 83–85, 131, 139, 142

    and salvation, 28

    and sin, 179

    and tradition, 5

holy water, 104, 152–53

Homily, 105, 123

homosexuality, 213–14

hope, 169, 171, 184–86, 244

human body, 205–7

    glorification of, 42

    image of God, 157, 205

    resurrection of, 42, 207

    and sexuality, 211–18

human life, 201

    purpose of, 25

    respect for, 201–210

human person, 20

dignity of, 21–22,
157–162
human race
first parents of, 22–24
gifts of, 22–23
sin of, 23–24
human trafficking, 202
humility, 169, 244, 250

I

idolatry, 183, 188
ignorance, 165, 179
immigration, 221
imprimatur, 57
incest, 203, 217
indifferentism, 190
indulgences, 127–29
infertility, 215–16
infidelity, 190, 217
information, right to, 229–30
intercessions, 244
irreligion, 189
Isaiah, 7
Israel, 7, 25, 134, 140, 194

J

Jeremiah, 7
Jesus Christ, 8, 28–44, 249
and Anointing of the
Sick, 130–33
Ascension of, 42–43, 99,
237–38

and Baptism, 83
birth of, 35
body of, 32
death, of 28, 39–41, 47,
99, 158, 248
disciples of, 39, 46, 160,
225–26
divinity of, 31, 37–38
as founder of Church,
235
as fullness of revelation,
5, 25
as Head of Church, 43,
50, 53, 135
and Holy Eucharist,
96–103
and Holy Orders, 134–39
human knowledge of, 32
humanity of, 31–32
and hypostatic union, 31
Incarnation of, 28, 30, 33
infancy of, 35–36
and liturgy, 75–78
as Lord, 30
and Matrimony, 140–49
as Messiah, 29, 36
miracles of, 37
as model of virtues, 30,
37
name of, 29, 191–92
and New Testament, 8
obedience of, 36
passion of, 36, 41, 158

preparation for his coming, 33
priestly, prophetic, and royal office of, 11, 29, 57, 135
as prophet, 38
and redemption, 24, 28, 39–43, 75, 129, 140, 196, 248
and religious life, 60
resurrection of, 28, 38, 41–42, 99, 158
and sacrament of Penance, 117–124
and sacraments, 80–81
Sacred Heart of, 32
as Savior, 29–30
Second Coming of, 43, 70
Son of God, 29–30
as teacher, 39
and Ten Commandments, 183, 190, 194, 197, 201, 211, 218, 225, 231, 234
John Paul II, 57, 157
John the Baptist, 33, 36
Joseph, St., 35, 238
Joshua, 7
joy, 173
judgment, 66–67, 70
justice, 167–68, 219
social, 220–24

K

killing, 201–9
kindness, 173
kingdom of God, 70, 170, 250
knowledge, 172–73
Kyrie, 103–4

L

laity, 57–58
Lamb of God, 101–8
last judgment, 44
Latin rite, 109, 138, 142
law
civil, 165, 200
moral, 163
lectern, 114
lector, 114
Lent, 77–78, 104, 153, 237
liberality, 169
lies, 226–28
liturgical vessels and vestments, 112–16
liturgical year, 76–8, 151, 237
liturgy, 75–78, 237, 244
and music and art, 76
and Word of God, 76, 105
Liturgy of the Eucharist, 106–8
Liturgy of the Hours, 76, 151
Liturgy of the Word, 105–6
Lord's Day, 194–97
Lord's Prayer, 108, 133, 154, 248–52, 257

love of God, 182–3, 185, 244
lust, 178, 212

M

Magisterium, 55
marriage, 212, 214, 217
    mixed, 144
    same-sex, 213–14
    See also Matrimony
martyr, 63, 226, 122
Mary, Blessed Virgin, 191, 253
    Annunciation to, 29, 33
    Assumption of, 71,
      237–38
    feasts of, 77, 237–38
    Immaculate Conception
      of, 24, 34, 237–38
    Mother of Church, 64
    Mother of God, 34,
      237–38
    Our Lady of Mount
      Carmel, 153
    virginity of, 34
mass media, 229–31
Mass. *See* Eucharistic Celebra-
    tion
masturbation, 212
Matrimony, 81, 137, 139–49,
    157, 187
    See also marriage
    Church law and, 143
    effects of, 145
    impediments to, 143–34

    indissolubility of, 145–46
    preparation for, 143
    purpose of, 140–41, 214
    and separation, 146
    sex outside of, 212, 217
    as a sign, 140, 142
    validity of, 143–48
medals, 128, 152–3
meditation, 246
memorial acclamation, or
    Mystery of Faith, 107
merit, 18, 40, 129, 158, 176,
    179
missionary, 59
modesty, 173, 233
monstrance, 112
morality, 158
    of acts, 161
    See also Ten Command-
      ments
Moses, 7, 181
mutilation, 202, 206–7
murder, 178, 202–4
mystery of Faith, 107

N

NaProTECHNOLOGY, 215
natural family planning, 214–15
natural law, 163
New Testament, 6, 8, 33, 105,
    134
NFP, 214–15
Nicene Creed, 10, 129

O

oaths, 191–3, 227
obedience, 61, 169, 187
Old Testament, 6–7
options, 116
Ordinary Time, 77–78
organ donation, 207
original justice, 23
original sin, 23–24, 83, 87, 158, 231
ownership, right of, 61, 220

P

pall, 115
palms, 152
parents, 57, 87, 91, 143, 164, 197–200
    duties to children, 199
    respect for, 198–99
parish, 56
Paschal Mystery, 43, 77, 101, 150
passions, 161, 176
pastor, 56
paten, 116
patience, 169, 173, 244
Paul, St., 182
peace, 173, 209
penance, 119, 121, 236, 238, 240
Penance and Reconciliation,
    sacrament of, 26, 81,
    117–124, 237

    effects of, 117–18, 120, 124
    seal of, 120, 228
    sign of, 118
penitent, 118–19
Penitential Act, 103–4
Pentecost, 78, 99
People of God, 48–50, 114
perjury, 193, 227
perseverance, 244
Peter, St., 38, 48, 52, 54
petition, 244, 249
piety, 169, 172–73
Pius IX, 34
Pius XII, 71
polygamy, 148, 217
Pope, 43, 46, 48, 52–8, 63, 107, 121, 128, 136, 236, 245
    infallibility of, 53
    primacy of, 52
pornography, 205, 213
    on–line, 233
poverty, 61, 187
    of heart 235
praise, 244
prayer, 164, 176, 186, 236, 243–53
    communal, 245, 247
    forms of, 245–48
    sentiments of, 244
    sources of, 244
    types of, 244, 246

prayer of the faithful, or Universal Prayer, 105, 107

precepts of the Church, 124–25, 236–40, 265

preface (of the Mass), 106

presumption, 179, 184–85

pride, 178, 209

priesthood. *See* Holy Orders

priests, 134–39
    and Anointing of the Sick, 130, 133
    and Confirmation, 92
    and Eucharist, 102
    and sacrament of Penance, 120–21
    and sacraments, 137

Preface Acclamation (Sanctus), 106

Presentation and Preparation of the Gifts, 106

profanity, 192

Profession of Faith, 10, 105, 170

prophecy, 7, 38

prostitution, 213

prudence, 167–8, 229

Psalms, 244

punishment, 127

purgatory, 66, 68–70, 129, 245, 248

purificator, 116

purity of heart, 232–35

R

rape, 203, 213

rash judgment, 227

reason, 3–4

redemption, 39, 247–48
    See also Jesus Christ

reincarnation, 66

relics, 114, 152, 190

religion, 169

religious life. *See* consecrated life

reproductive technology, 215–16

Responsorial Psalm, 105

restitution, 219, 224, 229

resurrection final, 71, 207

revelation, 3, 5, 6, 169
    and Jesus, 5, 25
    necessity of, 5

rights, 188, 202–3, 207, 219–21, 229

Rite for Blessing and Sprinkling of Water, 103–4

Roman Missal, 116

rosary, 128, 154, 253, 261–62

S

Sabbath, 21, 194

sacramentals, 150–54

sacraments, 26, 51, 79–149, 151
    and grace, 79, 141
    ministers of, 80, 92
    and Orthodox, 58

sacraments of initiation. *See* Baptism, Confirmation, Eucharist

Sacred Scripture. *See* Scripture

Sacred Tradition, 5–6

sacrifice, 186

sacrilege, 183, 189

saints, 62–3, 67, 153

salvation, 51, 165, 253
  and non–Christians, 86

salvation history, 29

sanctuary lamp, 112

scandal, 136, 185, 204–5, 213

scapulars, 152–53

schism, 63

scientific evidence, 4

Scripture, 17, 25, 43, 105, 163, 191, 244
  Books of, 6–7, 268–69
  differences, 10
  inspiration of, 7
  interpretation of, 9, 26
  parts of, 6–8
  Sacred, 6–10

secrets, 228–29

secular institute, 62

self-control, 167, 173

self-defense, 207–8

sexuality, 211–18

sign of the cross, 152, 247, 257

Sign of Peace, 108

simony, 189

sin, 23, 39–40, 119, 158, 195, 251
  actual, 175–80
  capital sins, 177
  forgiveness of, 83, 117–18
  mortal, 122, 164, 175–77, 180, 218
  occasions of, 179
  responsibility for, 202–3
  social sins, 180
  and temptation, 174
  venial, 123, 150, 165, 175, 177, 218

slander, 227

social justice, 220–21

situation ethics, 180

sloth, 178, 185

solidarity, 220

soul, human, 65, 157
  creation of, 21
  immortality of, 4, 26, 42

spouses, 139–49

State, the, 203, 215

statues, 153

stealing, 218–19

sterilization, 202, 206, 215

stole, 113

strikes, 222

suicide, 202–6

Sunday. *See* Lord's Day

superstition, 152, 188

supplication, 186

T

tabernacle, 111
talebearing, 228
tattoo, 206
temperance, 167–8, 174, 219, 232
temptation, 19–20, 174, 176, 233, 251
Ten Commandments, 7, 124, 181–240, 264
terrorism, 207
thanksgiving, 244
theology of the body, 157
torture, 202, 204, 207
Tradition, 5–6, 26
transubstantiation, 98–99
trial marriage, 217
truthfulness, 169, 225–31

U–W

Understanding, 172
Universal Prayer or Prayer of the Faithful, 105, 107
Vatican City, 53
Vatican Council, Second, 49, 109, 236

vestments, 112–13
Viaticum, 111, 133
vicar general, 56
virginity, 141
virtues, 46, 167–74, 199
    cardinal, 92, 167
    moral, 167, 169
    theological, 92, 167, 169–72
vocation, 199
vows, 60–61, 187–88, 191, 193
    of marriage, 142, 187
war, 208–9
water, Rite of Blessing and Sprinkling, 103–4
wisdom, 172
word of God, 6, 55, 76
work, 222
workers, 222
works of mercy, 159, 172, 266
worship, 186, 195–97
wrath, 178

BOOKS & MEDIA

A mission of the Daughters of St. Paul

As apostles of Jesus Christ, evangelizing today's world:

We are CALLED to holiness
by God's living Word and Eucharist.

We COMMUNICATE the Gospel message
through our lives and through all
available forms of media.

We SERVE the Church
by responding to the hopes and needs
of all people with the Word of God,
in the spirit of St. Paul.

For more information visit our website: www.pauline.org.

BOOKS & MEDIA

The Daughters of St. Paul operate book and media centers at the following addresses. Visit, call, or write the one nearest you today, or find us at www.pauline.org

CALIFORNIA
3908 Sepulveda Blvd, Culver City, CA 90230	310-397-8676
935 Brewster Avenue, Redwood City, CA 94063	650-369-4230
5945 Balboa Avenue, San Diego, CA 92111	858-565-9181

FLORIDA
145 S.W. 107th Avenue, Miami, FL 33174	305-559-6715

HAWAII
1143 Bishop Street, Honolulu, HI 96813	808-521-2731
Neighbor Islands call:	866-521-2731

ILLINOIS
172 North Michigan Avenue, Chicago, IL 60601	312-346-4228

LOUISIANA
4403 Veterans Memorial Blvd, Metairie, LA 70006	504-887-7631

MASSACHUSETTS
885 Providence Hwy, Dedham, MA 02026	781-326-5385

MISSOURI
9804 Watson Road, St. Louis, MO 63126	314-965-3512

NEW YORK
64 W. 38th Street, New York, NY 10018	212-754-1110

PENNSYLVANIA
Philadelphia—relocating	215-676-9494

SOUTH CAROLINA
243 King Street, Charleston, SC 29401	843-577-0175

VIRGINIA
1025 King Street, Alexandria, VA 22314	703-549-3806

CANADA
3022 Dufferin Street, Toronto, ON M6B 3T5	416-781-9131

¡También somos su fuente para libros,
videos y música en español!